HowExpert Presents

Professional Tennis Player 101

A Quick Guide on How to Become the Best Tennis Player You Can Be and Achieve Your Dreams of Becoming a Professional From A to Z

HowExpert with Christopher Morris

For more tips related to this topic, visit www.HowExpert.com/tennis.

Recommended Resources

- HowExpert.com – Quick 'How To' Guides on All Topics by Everyday Experts.
- HowExpert.com/books – HowExpert Books
- HowExpert.com/products – HowExpert Products
- HowExpert.com/courses – HowExpert Courses
- HowExpert.com/clothing – HowExpert Clothing
- HowExpert.com/membership – Learn All Topics from A to Z by Real Experts.
- HowExpert.com/affiliates – HowExpert Affiliate Program
- HowExpert.com/jobs – HowExpert Jobs
- HowExpert.com/writers – Write About Your #1 Passion/Knowledge/Expertise.
- YouTube.com/HowExpert – Subscribe to HowExpert YouTube.
- Instagram.com/HowExpert – Follow HowExpert on Instagram.
- Facebook.com/HowExpert – Follow HowExpert on Facebook.

Table of Contents

Introduction

So like all fans and casual watcher of tennis, you've seen Federer and Nadal on TV. You've enjoyed and endured Andy Murray's endless battles with Novak Djokovic. You've watched the Williams sisters, perhaps the most formidable and intimidating athletes ever to play the game. And you've seen, and heard, Sharapova at close quarters.

And you think you might be good enough to join them, or that you could coach your boy or girl to play as well as these legends of the game. Well, let's step into that dream world for a moment, and, to quote George from Seinfeld, I'll show you what it's like.

Unsurprisingly, you can't just walk into Wimbledon and start fencing with Federer. You have to earn your dues on the Challenger circuit. This involves considerably less household names, significantly less salubrious locations, and inordinately less income.

While Federer's most pressing fiscal challenge is keeping track of his complimentary Rolexes, things are a little bit different amid the grassroots of the professional game. Stories of professional tennis players sleeping in airports due to the lack of earnings even circulate, and you can just as easily find yourself grinding out results in front of the proverbial one man and his dog in Kazakhstan, as gliding over the manicured lawns of SW19.

Nonetheless, for your first sojourn into the professional game, you find yourself not too far from Wimbledon. The Roehampton Futures event is a fixture in the tennis calendar in Britain, and although its SW15 postcode isn't as well-known as that of Wimbledon, it's close enough for you to feel that you're just a step away from breaking into the big time.

Your opponent today will be Andrew Richardson. A little background reading on Richardson tells you that he's never been ranked in the world's top 100 players. He's also never qualified for a Grand Slam tournament, except when being handed a wildcard at Wimbledon (a common scenario among British players, who can count themselves fortunate that there is indeed a Grand Slam tournament in the UK).

In fact, Richardson has only managed to play 20 matches on the main ATP Tour, having spent the vast majority of his time churning out results, with mixed success, on the Challenger circuit. After the 20 ATP matches that he has played, his record reads rather unflatteringly 6-14, and two of those six wins were during one Wimbledon campaign.

In short, if Richardson hadn't been granted a wildcard to the 1997 Wimbledon Gentlemen's Singles, during which he was fortunate enough to run into two Spanish clay court specialists, one of whom was never ranked in the top 300 in the world, he would only have won four matches on the ATP Tour in his entire career, while losing 13.

Not exactly a CV to rival Roger and Rafa.

So as you begin your professional tennis journey you're feeling quietly confident. Richardson has dropped down to the Futures in one last attempt to relaunch his career, and he has never exactly being a top class player, so this should be a great opportunity for someone on an upward curve to make a good beginning in the game.

When you first encounter Richardson, though, you are slightly taken aback by his sheer size. He must be 6' 7" at least, and towers over you at the net. Still, during the warmup you manage to get your forehand going nicely; your best stroke and a source of pride in your game. You feel in good form and ready to go, and are not even slightly discouraged by losing the toss. Richardson elects to serve, and you prepare yourself for your first game as a professional tennis player.

Thankfully, Richardson doesn't look anything like as intimidating from a distance, in fact it's easy to forget that he's particularly tall. He winds up and begins his left-handed service motion, and your senses heighten in anticipation of receiving...thunk! The ball flies past you at a rate of knots, appearing more like a yellowish blur than a spherical object, and crashes unceremoniously into the mesh tennis club fencing. 15-0.

You try not to worry too much about the fact that you barely moved when facing Richardson's first serve, and steel yourself to do better the second time. However, this is the first time that you've looked at his service motion and ball toss from the advantage court, and you realize too late that your opponent has gone for the sliding serve wide to your backhand; often a favourite of left-handers, and particularly associated with the great John McEnroe. Stretching every sinew, you just about manage to get a racquet frame on the ball, but this is nowhere near sufficient to return the serve. 30-0.

Back to the deuce court, and this time you are ready for Richardson's serve. You guess correctly and look to block the rising ball back into court with your trusted forehand. But although you manage to get the center of your strings on the ball, the sheer force of the notoriously heavy ball that big servers deliver jolts your racquet head, twisting it our of your control. It feels like trying to return a concrete block, rather than a tennis ball. Your return limply fades into the net. 40-0.

While there seems little to lose at 40-0 down, you feel keen to at least get the ball back in court and get into the game. Fortunately, Richardson narrowly misses with a scything strike down the middle, which would otherwise have been an ace by miles. Finally, you get to look at a second serve. This is delivered at a somewhat more sedate pace - although Richardson's second serve still exceeds 100mph in speed - and you see it pretty well.

Then it lands on the concrete court, and spits venomously at you, elevating rapidly from the topspin that Richardson has expertly applied to his kick serve. By the time it reaches you it's at the height of your head. You manage to block it back reasonably well with your backhand, and begin to move back towards the center of the court. As you make this movement, you can already see Richardson scurrying towards the ball, utilizing short, distinctive split steps. With an almost spiteful swish of his racquet, your opponent whips a topspin forehand right back from where you came, wrong footing you completely, and comfortably holding his serve.

As the match unfolds, you begin to appreciate just how accomplished your opponent is, and begin to feel somewhat inadequate; indeed, you feel every inch the seven inches shorter than him that you actually are. You're beginning to understand how this guy became the British number 2 behind Tim Henman.

He hits the ball 10mph harder than you, his serve is like a rocket, he never seems to be behind in a point. Richardson is a similar height to such familiar professional players as Marin Cilic, John Isner, Juan Marin del Potro, and, the most successful sever of all-time, Ivo Karlovic. It feels as if the ball is being fired at you from a cannon, before rearing up with the ferocity and vigor of a kicking horse.

When you do get the ball into court, Richardson is superbly consistent. He knows that he has every chance of holding his own serve time and again, and plays much more consistently in your service games, like the seasoned pro that he is. Although you have your moments on your own serve, and even manage to earn a couple of break points once you've adjusted to the sheer pace of the Richardson service, the first set slips away 2-6. You're beginning to wonder how good the 14 people who beat him are.

As you acclimatize to the class of your opponent, you make a better fist of the second set. You hold serve several times, and manage to land a few telling blows with your pride-and-joy forehand. You expect Richardson to buckle under the pressure as you lead 1-0, 2-1, 3-2 and 4-3, perhaps forgetting that he's played in the last 32 at Wimbledon, and against numerous better players than you.

He imperiously holds serve to level at 4-4, and now the pressure is right back on you. Realizing that this is the business end of the set, you vow to play aggressively and put it right back on him. With this thought still ringing around your brain, you hit a blistering forehand winner that paints the line to go 15-0...wait, it's been called out. You're really annoyed, and compel the umpire to overrule. But he's miles away from the line, and can't reasonably do so. And there's no Hawkeye here, sunshine.

Piqued by the previous point, you then double fault, and soon you're facing two break points. You haven't faced a break point all set, but now these are virtual match points. Thankfully, you nail your first serve and force what will surely be a defensive shot from Richardson. But, to your surprise, he feels secure enough at this point to have a swing at your serve, figuring that he has nothing to lose. He nails it. The ball comes back at you with interest cross court, and you have absolutely no hope of returning it.

Two minutes later you're shaking hands. Game, set and match Richardson - 6-2, 6-4. Perhaps the Challenger circuit isn't going to be the elementary stepping stone to greatness that you imagined.

*   *   *   *

The reason that I know what it's like to face a run-of-the-mill yet extremely talented tennis professional such as Andrew Richardson is that I was part of the same LTA development squad as him, in Lincolnshire, United Kingdom, for several years. Trust me, even to get to his level, which was a peak world ranking of 133, is far from easy. It requires a lot of dedication, practice, hard work, self-belief, athleticism, mental toughness, and technical skill.

There are at least 500 strong professional players out there. They are all hungry. Very few of them are rich. It doesn't matter if they come from Bulgaria, Belgium, Bolivia or Botswana...they will be good. Extremely good.

Just to underline this point, the rank outsider Marcus Willis created a media storm in 2017, by qualifying for Wimbledon. In doing so, he beat the highly regarded teenager Andrey Rublev (ranked 32 in the world at the time of writing), and then eliminated Ričardas Berankis at the All England Club. This earned Willis a dream match-up with the legendary Roger Federer on Centre Court. And although Willis had absolutely no hope of winning this match, he performed perfectly creditably, with the last two sets having the very respectable scoreline of 3-6, 4-6.

Willis was world ranked 772 at the time. That's how many good players there are out there.

The top 50 in the world, where the really money is, are almost ridiculously good. To get to that level you have to be probably the best player that your country has produced in any 5-year period. You must be in supreme physical shape. You have to possess mental resilience. And, unlike other sports, you can't have weaknesses. If you have weaknesses then they will be exploited. Even the 20-time Grand Slam champion has had the tiny vulnerabilities on his backhand side exposed, so you'd better believe your weaknesses will be exposed.

Many junior Grand Slam winners and world number ones have failed to make it on the ATP Tour. The likes of The likes of Florin Mergea, Todd Reid, Roman Valent, Carlos Cuadrado, Julien Jeanpierre, Clement Morel, Brydan Klein, Daniel Elsner all won junior Grand Slams, yet their names hardly read like a roll call of the illuminati of the tennis world!

That's the bad news. The good news is that anyone with a modicum of coordination can play excellent tennis, and with considerable determination and practice can even reach professional standard. Achieving mastery in any field is all about practice, and if you doubt this for a second then you should check out a video on YouTube which features a completely table tennis player practising the game with diligence for one hour every single day. By the end of the video, this previously completely uncoordinated individual is capable of playing tournament-standard table tennis. That's after just 12 months' practice.

If you are willing to invest several years in improving your tennis then you can go further than even this. All professional players have been through thousands of hours of systematic practice in order to develop their skills. And the techniques required in order to develop the appropriate qualities are now well-established, meaning that anyone can gain access to professional-standard tennis, without the weighty resources that were necessary in the past.

I was fortunate enough to work with many of the top coaches in the LTA in England, and have also played with numerous professional players, both male and female. Equally, I am aware of some of the pitfalls and problems that ambitious tennis players may encounter.

While the information is out there in terms of coaching, practice, and the elements required to excel at tennis, there is a lot of bluster and misinformation available as well. Oh, and some of this comes from what are considered very reputable sources as well, making developing as a tennis player something of a minefield.

So the aim of this book will be to provide a template for any player to seriously improve their game, and to even go as far as playing professional-standard tennis should they feel passionate enough about the game in order to invest the time and effort required.

The text will go through some of the drills and techniques involved. But I don't want this to be the sole focus of this book, as there are many other titles which focus on these obvious aspects of the game. Instead, I want to convey my experience of playing good standard tennis to you, express the ethos which I consider to be important, and inform you of some of the things you can expect to encounter if you intend to play tennis professional level.

There is a lot more to tennis than simply hitting a ball, and this book will help guide you around some of the many obstacles that are inevitable.

Chapter 1 – Making the First Steps in Tennis

Rome wasn't built in a day. We all have to start somewhere. Even multiple Grand Slam champions began in their local club, playing thoroughly unimpressive tennis. Some have more natural talent than others, but with practice anyone can become competent.

However, you should also bear in mind that the game of tennis is very difficult, and you will almost certainly find it extremely tricky at first. Most people that take their first steps onto a tennis court struggle to hit the ball over the net and in the court at first, which is why it is often asserted that you should begin at a very young age if you have any intention of playing seriously. There aren't too many examples of professional players who didn't begin at a tender age, that's for sure.

Another thing that shouldn't discourage as you make your first steps in tennis is your level of natural ability. I personally ended up playing tennis seriously, as it was discovered at school that I had an unusual level of natural talent. I could actually rally the ball back and forth with my teacher as many times as everyone else in the class put together. But although I may have had a head start on others, I also believe that it is easily possible for absolutely anyone to reach the level that I was at in those early days. And reasonably quickly.

The most important thing to remember as you embark on your tennis playing journey is that the game is ultimately supposed to be fun. In common with most competitive endeavors it is often taken extremely seriously, but ultimately you shouldn't forget that you are only engaging in a bat and ball game. Try to enjoy your time on the court, particularly when you're just beginning, and take something positive out of every experience, regardless of whether you win or lose.

This chapter will encompass the following:

- Selecting appropriate equipment;

- Selecting the best racquet for your age and ability;

- What age you should start playing at;

- Basic grips, etc.

- What tennis activity you should be involved in when you first start.

How to Choose the Best Tennis Equipment

There is no doubt that your racquet is the most important aspect of tennis equipment, but we will briefly begin by discussing other aspects of your kit. Firstly, specialist tennis shoes are available for various court conditions, and it is certainly worth considering these if you have a suitable budget. However, a good all-purpose tennis shoe will suffice for all surfaces.

It is also worth considering that clay courts are particularly hard on shoes, and this can be a concern for parents in particular. It is also debatable whether clay is the ideal surface to develop as a young player, as it can encourage attritional play. Having said that, modern tennis is undoubtedly dominated by baseline play, and clay arguably provides the ideal opportunity to mold consistency in this department, while also aiding the development of stamina.

Nonetheless, unless you are resident in a European country in which clay courts are de rigueur, it is probably sensible to begin playing on hard courts. These require less specialist shoes than either grass or clay, are not as hard wearing as clay in particular, and are available all-year-round.

Tennis clothing shouldn't be too tight, but loose fitting garments have become rather unfashionable recently. In all honesty, it really makes little difference to how you play, and children can afford to wear larger clothing that will last them longer.

More important are the balls that you play with initially. While there is always a tendency to mimic the professionals, it is probably more advisable for young players to get their hands on the fastest balls available. Different balls from varying manufacturers do feature differing air pressure, and this affects the speed with which they travel through the court. Young players will be encouraged by the higher pressure balls, as they will initially find it difficult to get the ball through the court with any pace.

However, the racquet that you use is obviously the most important item of tennis equipment. Selecting this is really dependent on age and ability. But let's start at the start. When beginning your tennis playing journey, it is important to select a racquet with a sizeable sweet spot. There are plenty of racquets available that effectively do the work for you, meaning that when you do strike the ball in the middle of the strings, you will attain power more easily.

Getting the racquet head size right for younger players can be a balancing act. It is certainly not advisable for the younger player to use the size of racquet that is utilized by the world's best ever player. Roger Federer uses a Wilson staff with a tiny racquet head, although his previous equipment featured an even smaller head than this!

On the other hand, although there are racquets available with huge racquet heads, younger players may find these too heavy and ultimately unwieldy. Don't underestimate the danger of causing physical discomfort with a tennis racquet; there is a reason that the complaint tennis elbow exists. Indeed, this condition is a serious risk with heavier racquets, while the lightest equipment on the market will force players to use their wrists a great deal, and ultimately place a huge amount of strain on them.

To illustrate this problem, I recently played with Federer's racquet for the first time, having been more accustomed to heavier racquets with larger sweet spots. While the Federer Pro Staff enables a huge amount of control and feel, I knew within 20 minutes of using it for the first time that it wasn't for me. Indeed, by the end of the two-hour session, my wrist was barely able to move! So be very careful when selecting a racquet for a child, as the developing body will struggle if their racquet is not sufficiently powerful.

Nonetheless, I wouldn't recommend a racquet that weighs over 300 grammes for younger players, as it will simply be too heavy. A shorter grip is also recommended for beginners, with 4 1/8 or 4 2/8 advisable. Oh, and definitely don't forget a tension dampener. They are widely available for next to nothing, and will make playing the game considerably less stressful on your wrists.

Finally, there are now many junior tennis racquets available on the market. I personally never used one of these, but then I didn't begin playing tennis on a full-sized courted till the age of eight. Many young players graduate to lawn tennis at a significantly more tender age than this, and for these individuals it is certainly sensible to utilize these stumpier racquets.

What Age Should You Start Playing Tennis?

However, I question the wisdom of playing on a full-size tennis court with adult equipment at the age of three or four. While many great players began very young, they didn't necessarily play in adult conditions for several years. I myself began by playing short tennis with a plastic racquet and sponge ball, and I feel that this is a much better way to learn the basic techniques and tactics of the game.

Short tennis is now also often referred to as mini tennis, and I definitely believe that this is the best place for youngsters to start. It will be rather discouraging for young children to play on a full-size court at a pre-school age, and mini tennis enables players to gain a degree of proficiency in a short period of time. Striking the sponge ball is considerably easier than dealing with a proper tennis ball, and the dimensions of a mini tennis courts certainly suit the developing body.

Another valuable and enjoyable aspect of your early tennis career is the opportunity to play lots of mixed tennis with girls and boys. Until the age of approximately 10, there is little difference in tennis-playing proficiency between boys and girls, with the best players of both genders playing at a roughly similar level. At around this age, Serena Williams infamously beat Andy Roddick, and I remember playing close matches with top female players when I was younger.

This means that young players can participate in mixed and social tennis, which will benefit their development as a person as well as their tennis skills. This can also be a useful precursor to participating in mixed doubles, and other social events, later in a tennis career.

Speaking of doubles, I would strongly advise very young players to participate in this variant of tennis, as well as singles. In fact, it is debatable whether young players should really be playing competitively at all, and certainly not in tournaments. I played in my first short tennis tournament when I was seven years old, and I think any competitive action at a younger age than this is counter-productive and unnecessary.

Learning the basic techniques of the game and having fun should certainly be the priority at first. It can be difficult to quell the natural competitiveness of some youngsters, and I know that I always greatly relished competition from a young age. But keeping them away from tournaments for a few years at least will be beneficial, as it will prevent them from being discouraged by losing to superior players.

I was fortunate to have some natural talent, and reached the national short tennis finals just six months after picking up a racquet for the first time. But this won't be the journey for all players, and any boy or girl's ultimate success in the game will certainly not be predicated on these very early gambits.

But doubles should be considered a vital part of any player's tennis education. Spending time at the net will lead to a more rounded technique, and this will stand any player in good stead for their later career. Net play is arguably less important now than it was in the past, but anyone who develops volleying skills will have a useful string to their bow, while doubles is also a key aspect of social tennis, and another option in the professional game.

At the age of 41, as I am while writing this, I have stopped playing singles almost entirely, because it's just more fun to play doubles. I'm sure singles will become even less fun in the years to come! Thus, if you intend to spend your life participating in the sport it is better to become accustomed to doubles at an early age.

The Most Important Basic Techniques

There is not going to be a huge amount of material in this book regarding how to hit a tennis ball, although I will go over all of the basic techniques, and the strokes and techniques that you need to learn as you get better. But I don't want to devote vast amounts of material to technical issues. There are three reasons for this. Firstly, this information is already widely available. Secondly, this is an area of the sport that will be conveyed by coaches, and will be based partly on observation of the individual player's technique.

Thirdly, the only way to learn how to hit a tennis ball is to practice your shots over and over and over again. Whilst some players will exhibit natural talent, the groundstrokes, serve, volleys and overheads absolutely cannot be developed without continual repetition over several years. While the basic techniques can be communicated to young players, it is almost impossible to truly teach someone how to hit a tennis ball. There is so much feel involved in this, and this can really only be developed over thousands and thousands and thousands of strikes.

Ultimately, there is no right or wrong way to play tennis, and thus it is difficult to give blanket advice with regard to the actual strokes. However, some basic principles can be finalized, along with the racquet grips available. We will look at some more advanced techniques in the next chapter.

Serving begins with the ball toss. This is really the central aspect of the service motion. Even if you're the world's greatest server, you won't hit your service well if you don't get the ball toss right. Indeed, you will often notice that professional players who are struggling with their service motions, or just generally nervous, will repeatedly get their ball toss wrong. Laura Robson would be a good recent example.

Thus, practicing the ball toss on a regular basis is particularly valuable, especially when you're starting out as a tennis player. The ball toss should be slightly out in front of you for most services, although it needs to be behind you for the kick serve. We will deal with the technique for this aspect of the game later in the book.

One thing that you should always be thinking when you serve is to reach the racquet head as high as possible. This gives you increased height to get the ball over the net and downwards into the service box, and also potentially as leverage. Similarly, you should ideally jump slightly up in the air to meet your ball task as you serve, or at least begin by getting on your tiptoes. Every inch counts when delivering the service.

An interesting strategy with the service is to move around the baseline when you are delivering the serve. You can actually make the 'down the T' serve so much easier by standing right next to the center line, and if you do this surreptitiously then you can catch your opponent so that they don't even notice your altered service position.

Similarly, it is valuable to learn how to hit a wide variety of different services from the same ball toss. Roger Federer is a notorious master of this facet of the game. There are sliders, sliced services, power serves, wide serves, centrally positioned serves, and body serves to learn, and if you can hit as many of these with the same motion and ball toss as possible, it will hide your intention from your opponent, making it far more difficult to return your service.

With groundstrokes, the absolute key to hitting them effectively is to take your racquet back as early as possible. This is an important part of preparation, and it is good to drill yourself in this technique from as early in your tennis career as possible, as it will become essential when people start hitting the ball hard at you.

You should certainly have taken your racquet right back by the time that the ball arrives in your half of the court, at least for an ordinary groundstroke. If you are chasing down a drop shot down this obviously doesn't apply.

Another key movement with groundstrokes is to begin low and finish high. It is also important to move your legs, and especially knees, properly. You should be bending down to meet lower bouncing balls, otherwise you will never hit them properly.

It's also important to get into the right position to hit the tennis ball, and that means never getting too close to the ball. Many shots that are not executed correctly, even in the professional game, come about due to the player either being too close or too far away from the ball. Obviously, this position should be roughly a racquet length away from the ball, but the only way to learn this is perpetual practice.

Finally, the follow-through is incredibly important in all tennis strokes, but particularly the groundstrokes. You shouldn't poke or prod at the ball, you should hit right through each ball and swing the racquet thoroughly after making contact. You will see with top class players that their follow-through is as important, and probably even longer, than their backlift. Watch the way that Rafael Nadal unwinds his racquet, for example.

When volleying, you should take a much shorter swing at the ball, often described as punching. The exception to this is when you're taking the ball out of the air from deeper in the court with a drive volley, which involves taking the ball from below the height of the net, and effectively hitting a groundstroke-type shot with topspin. For drive volleys you must hit through the ball with significant whip, otherwise you will end up hitting it miles out of court.

But for standard volleys, you don't really need to hit the ball too hard, and the stroke should be based around a short, punchy motion. It's also really important to steer the ball by manipulating the racquet head when volleying, as you will be a sitting duck within a few strokes if you don't finish the point while at the net.

Finally, the smash or overhead is the most dramatic shot in the game, and probably the most satisfying when executed correctly. The first thing I would say about the smash is that you should always be willing to let the ball drop. It is more satisfying taking it out of the air, and this can also be the right shot. But take into account the trajectory of the ball and your court position, and quite frequently you might find that you can deliver a powerful overhead and accurate overhead without taking the ball out of the air.

Secondly, don't overhit when hitting a smash. If you catch the ball decently, you will almost always win the point with an overhead. Always keep an eye on the court position of your opponent, and this can lead to an easy put away. Finally, it is important to hit smashes and overhead shots in a downward trajectory, as if you power the ball from this position and fail to do so, the ball will almost without exception go beyond the baseline.

Gripping the racquet

So, finally, I want to look at the grips you should be using for the various strokes. There are a huge amount available, with names such as continental, chopper, hammer, eastern, western and semi-western all bamboozling the beginner. Each of these grips has advantages and disadvantages, but I want to look at the grips that I advocate, rather than the other grips, and explain the reasons for this.

For the forehand, the semi-western grip has become probably the most popular approach in tennis. This is because it enables players to hit with significant amounts of topspin, while also not being too extreme in nature. This first point is going to be extremely important as your game develops, and I'm a big advocate of doing the right thing with your tennis from day one, rather than trying to make the game easy for beginners.

For the semi-western grip, you should look to grip the racquet as close to the base as possible. This allows maximum leverage and power. If you hold a tennis racquet for the first time, you may notice that the handle is split into eight equal sections. The semi-western grip involves placing the palm side of your index fingers knuckle against the bottom-right section if you're right-handed, and the bottom-left section if you are left-handed.

With the western grip, which also has its advocates, the hand is effectively underneath the racquet handle, which can be particularly uncomfortable and difficult for beginners. It also makes the transition into other strokes more fiddly. This is a big reason why the semi-western grip should be utilized, although switching to volleying with this approach can still be a little tricky.

The semi-western grip results in the racquet face pointing towards the ground, meaning that it is easier to brush up and over the ball to produce topspin. This is absolutely essential if you have any pretentions whatsoever of becoming a decent tennis player.

You really won't go anywhere in the game by hitting the ball flat, although tennis can still be a fun sport to participate in, even if you're doing everything fundamentally wrong! Although learning to hit with topspin takes a bit of time and effort, I would argue that it even makes the game more fun for rookie players, as it increases your margins of error, ultimately making the game a lot less frustrating. It's all too easy to hit the ball out of the back of the court when hitting without spin, whereas topspin makes the ball dip into the court before the baseline.

For the service...yes, you're going to have to learn another grip! The serve requires a specialist grip, referred to as the continental grip, which enables you to hit with the variety that you will require for this stroke that starts every rally. The continental grip also makes it easier to flex your wrist at the point of impact, which will have a big impact on your service games.

In order to form the continental grip, it is simply necessary to effectively shake hands with the racquet, hence the fact that the continental grip is full so often described as the shake-hands grip. You should also volley using this grip, and it will furthermore provide the foundation for your backhand grip as well.

I'm not going to discuss the grip and technique for a one-handed backhand in this book, as I strongly advocate using two hands on the racquet. I love watching players with a one-handed backhand, particularly Roger Federer, but I firmly believe that it is simply more practical and consistent to hit with two hands.

When forming the two-handed grip for the backhand, you should begin with your stronger hand in the continental forehand grip. Then also utilize the same grip with your second hand, which is naturally placed above your stronger hand on the racquet handle. Your hands should be closely positioned against one another, without overlapping.

And, finally, when executing any tennis grip, it is important to keep your eyes trained on the ball at all times. Remember Forrest Gump playing ping pong!

So that's all of the basics converted that you need to play a proficient game of tennis. I should note that many coaches will advocate using simpler grips and techniques when first learning the game, and there is nothing wrong with this whatsoever. But if you're going to become a proficient player then you will need to use more sophisticated grips sooner or later, so I am a big advocate of making this sooner rather than later.

In the next chapter, we will look at more advanced tennis techniques.

Chapter 2 – Becoming an Intermediate Tennis Player

By now you should resemble something approaching a competent tennis player. Whether you yet feel qualified to describe yourself as a tennis player or not will remain on the vanity and confidence of the individual! But after around six to twelve months, you should be able to rally competently, hit the ball in the court with regularity, and enjoy a decent, competitive game of tennis with players of similar ability.

However, it is perfectly natural to want to improve at the game of tennis, and reach the next level. Of course, only a chosen few have the determination and persistence required to play professional-standard tennis. But there are many decent club players all over the world who derive a great deal of pleasure from tennis, while also playing the game with a good degree of skill and competitiveness.

It is far from impossible to become one of these people, but at this intermediate stage you should begin to think about directing your practice and approach to the game towards genuinely improving. Naturally, practice in itself will have a big impact on your standard of play, but the effectiveness of this practice and rapidity of your improvement will determine how much you do indeed improve.

With this in mind, this chapter will cover the following topics:

- What drills and practice routines you should use as a beginner;

- Whether or not you should play tennis variants;

- What are the key factors that make a good player;

- What are some of the mistakes that young players and coaches make;

- Should you use two hands on both sides when learning;

- When you should upgrade equipment, and to what.

The Best Drills and Routines to Improve Your Game

Tennis isn't necessarily the most affordable sport to play regularly, although I would suggest that it is cheaper than, for example, golf. However, you can make a great deal of progress as a tennis player without opposition, and even without a tennis court and net. I certainly spent a lot of time engaged in tennis drills outside of a tennis court.

And one is reminded of the greatest cricketer of all-time, Donald Bradman, who used to practice batting with a stick, rather than a cricket bat, and a marble, rather than a cricket ball. In short, don't let a lack of access to facilities discourage you. Bradman used to say that hitting a ball with a bat seemed a lot easier after trying to hit a marble with a stick.

There are several key tips that I'd like to convey to the budding tennis player here, and I'd like to begin with the value of wall practice. I spent literally hours practising both my groundstrokes and volleys against the garage wall of my house, and I firmly believe this this is the primary reason that I became a competent tennis player. The garage wall never missed! The ball always comes back, and it's a very simple way of developing consistent strokes.

Even when I graduated to play at a tennis club, there was always a wall available with a net chalked on it. I always took advantage of this facility, and I would strongly advise young players to understand and cherish the value of practising against a wall. While it is also important to get on a tennis court for several reasons, wall practice can still provide hours of valuable tennis tuition, without the need for any opposition or facilities.

Wall practice is particularly useful for volleys. There is a simple drill that you can utilize here. Volley from your forehand side so that the ball hits the wall and comes back to your forehand ten times. Then do the same with your backhand. Then volley from forehand to backhand, back to forehand, and so on. Do this twenty times. Then start again, and repeat, repeat, repeat. That's how to get good at volleying!

In accordance with this principle, the fantastic value of ball machines should also never be underestimated. Again, ball machines provide the opportunity to drill your groundstrokes, while never having to worry about the ball coming over the net from your opponent. Equally, ball machines can be set to provide all manner of different spins and speeds, meaning that you can practice a particular aspect of the game which is causing you difficulty.

There is no way of getting around this; every tennis player is only as good as the weakest aspect of the game. If you have a particular Achilles heel on the tennis court, you can be absolutely 100% certain that opponents will identify this rapidly, and exploit it ruthlessly. Therefore, tennis education should always be founded on improving your weaknesses up to an acceptable level, as much as developing your strengths. I had a weak backhand as a younger player, and spent many hours drilling this stroke until it reached a decent standard.

Ball machines can play a major part in this process, and they should be embraced by all serious tennis players, and particularly those learning the game.

Backhand Improvement

As I just mentioned, my backhand was definitely a weakness when I played competitively, and this brings us neatly onto the next topic. I believe that the backhand is of critical importance, and possibly even more so in junior tennis. You'll find that most professional players have probably devoted more attention to improving their backhands than any other stroke.

There are two primary reasons for this. Firstly, it is a difficult shot to grasp at first, as the movement of reversing your hand is just less natural than the forehand motion. If you struggle with the backhand at first, rest assured that many great players have also found the stroke difficult. Indeed, Roger Federer has stated that he gave up on trying to utilize a two-handed grip for his backhand as he simply could not execute the stroke with this approach.

Secondly, in junior tennis, I can tell you from personal experience, the backhand wing is frequently a serious weakness. This is because the only way to really develop the backhand is by lengthy and continuous practice drills. Very, very few tennis players have stepped on to a tennis court and instantly been good at hitting backhands. It is a tricky stroke, and as a young player you will gain a massive advantage over the opposition if you have a strong backhand.

So, in my opinion, if you have any intention of getting good at tennis, you should particularly concentrate on your backhand side. The ball machine can be utilized for this, although it is also good to work with the human opponents as well. But I recommend one very simple drill for improving the backhand, as I myself spent hours doing this as a young player.

Simply stand in the corner of the tennis court, and hit nothing but backgrounds for at least 30 minutes (I often did it for an hour). Hit one across court, and then hit the next shot down the line. Rinse and repeat. Do this thousands and thousands of times, and you are well on your way to becoming a competent tennis player!

Another thing that I should emphasize at this point is that you should learn to hit through the backhand from day one. I personally always found slicing the backhand much easier, and there are a few professional players who have adopted this as their primary stroke. It certainly didn't do Steffi Graf any harm, while Britain's Greg Rusedski, a US Open finalist, also primarily utilized a sliced backhand.

However, that isn't going to get you very far in this day and age, in my opinion, and every top class professional tennis player hits through the ball on the majority of backhands. So the sooner you accept that this is the way to hit this stroke, the sooner you can develop it, and the better player you will become.

Any serious young player who encounters an opponent with an almost exclusively sliced backhand will relentlessly target it. So be prepared! We will discuss the backhand again in more depth in a coming chapter.

After the backhand, it is absolutely critical to develop a strong service motion. Any decent service begins with a good ball toss, and it is therefore worthwhile to work on this extensively. one way to do this is to place your racquet face down on the ground, get into the service position, and practice landing the ball toss on the same spot of the racquet every single time. The ball toss should be somewhat out in front of you, so that you can lean your weight forwards when you serve.

Or, at least, this is how I believe that the serve should be done, although there are certain professional players that throw the ball behind themselves, while this is an advanced technique for the kick serve that we will develop later. But begin with the basics. Get your ball toss right, and you can go from there.

The only way to develop the service is simply to practice the motion over and over again. I have mentioned some of the basic technique for serving in the previous chapter, but it is also important to practice every single possible serve. Learn to hit with power, and also to slice the ball, using the grip mentioned in chapter 1. Develop a serve down the middle, a slider out wide, and an accurate body serve.

Place handkerchiefs on the court in several key service box positions, and attempt to land your service as close to these objects as possible. If you are left-handed, particularly concentrate on the deuce court, and if you are a right-hander particular concentrate on the advantage court, as these are the trickier positions depending on which hand that you use.

These are good basic drills for junior players to begin with. Obviously the forehand is a foundation of any player's game, and we will deal with that in the coming section. But pretty much everyone who picks up a tennis racquet can hit a forehand, and mastering the backhand and service in particular will stand you in very good stead as a developing tennis player.

Developing the Key Strokes

The foundation of any stronger tennis player is the topspin forehand. This is the most aggressive and point-scoring stroke in the game. If you don't have a decent topspin forehand, you'll never play tennis at anything approaching a high level. So it should be an absolute priority to develop this very early on in your development. Indeed, the first time I stepped on to a tennis court to hit a proper tennis ball with a full-sized racquets, I immediately was taught the topspin technique, and it felt great when I was quickly able to do this with some competence. (I should emphasize that I'd already played short tennis extensively at this time, and participated in the British finals).

The topspin aspect of the shot is important, as this causes the ball to dip, making it possible to hit with both power and accuracy.

When hitting the topspin forehand, it is generally advisable to have a semi-open stance. If you get too sideways-on then it will be impossible to satisfactorily rotate your body through the stroke. But if you are too face-on, you won't get the control required to hit the shot with accuracy.

As mentioned previously, all groundstrokes involve a bottom-to-top motion. Essentially, you are painting a rainbow with your racquet head. As you strike the ball, your feet should be reasonably spread apart at a width slightly less than your shoulders, although players will tend to find their own comfortable technique in this area. You should approach the ball with split steps, shorter physical steps to make it easier to remain on your toes for the next ball. We will discuss the split step drills in a later chapter.

Once you have taken the racquet back, you should then swing it in an upward motion from the low position, before striking the ball somewhere between waist and shoulder height. Of course, this isn't always possible depending on the nature of the point, but the overwhelming majority of forehands will be hit in this position.

You will know that you are getting the topspin motion correct, as when you brush up the back of the ball you will feel more friction and resistance than for a flat strike. You should make contact with the ball ideally when it is still marginally out in front of you in order to gain the maximum amount of power.

In order to maintain your balance, you should move your left arm across your body, so that it is held in a roughly parallel position. As you strike the ball, you should rotate your hips with the racquet, and also move the weight of your body from your right foot, which will be the back foot for the stroke (for right handers), and into your left foot.

As you strike through the ball, you also need to flick your wrist, in order to generate the topspin. This motion can only be mastered with trial and error, but it is almost invaluable to watch the great proponents of the topspin forehand in order to learn the technique. Watch how Federer and Nadal rotate their racquets as they strike the ball with their forehands, almost creating a flicking emotion despite the ferocity of the stroke.

You should follow through as far as possible with the racquet, but as soon as the stroke is complete you should also look to return to the central baseline position. Obviously this isn't universally the case, as sometimes you'll be heading forward to the net, but the point is that you should never stand still admiring your stroke. This is one of the big mistakes that amateurs make. As soon as you have hit the ball, even if you think it's a guaranteed winner, you should already be making your way into the appropriate court position.

The first thing to note about the backhand is that it is impossible to impart the same level of spin on the ball as it is with the forehand. It must be said that one advantage of the one-handed backhand is that it does allow more topspin to be applied, but I think the advantages of the two-hander outweigh this one issue.

All excellent backhands begin with a perfect initial position. You should split step heading into the stroke, and maintain a similar position and balance to the forehand stroke.

The backhand requires a fairly similar motion into the forehand, with the importance of taking the racquet back before following through still paramount. However, because there is less spin imparted by a two-handed backhand then a one-handed forehand, due to the impossibility of flicking the wrist as much, the stroke has a slightly different feel. There is definitely a steering element at times with the backhand that is rarely utilized with the forehand, and the backhand is also usually hit lower over the net, due to the relative lack of spin.

As you are hitting your backhand, you should turn your shoulders so that you can look over your dominant shoulder at the incoming ball. Again, weight transference from back to front foot is essential, but this will be the opposite of the forehand side.

Professional coaches will often tell you to 'stay with the shot' with both forehand and backhand. What this means is that the follow-through should be absolute, with your momentum continuing forwards even after the ball has left your racquet head. Extend your arms towards the ball during and after striking it. Your elbows should finish high when striking both the forehand and backhand.

You may also need to rotate your hips more for a cross court stroke, as opposed to a down the line effort. Furthermore, when hitting the ball down the line, it sometimes helps to catch the ball slightly on the outer portion of the racquet head, rather than slap bang in the middle. This technique allows you to create the angle, but it is quite an advanced approach, and certainly requires considerable practice.

While slice is sometimes used on the forehand side, it is extremely rare compared to the backhand slice. The backhand slice is an important part of any player's armory, as it can be used as a defensive weapon, and occasionally in an attacking sense as well.

Firstly, it is important to note that the slice is a one-handed stroke. It is also often employed to lower bouncing balls. It skids through when hitting the court, rather than leaping upwards as is the case with topspin shots.

The slice is very much a side-on shot as well. Your chest should be facing the sideline when you make contact with a slice. It is also not a top-to-bottom stroke as is the case with other groundstrokes. The slice begins at shoulder height, with the player wielding his racquet somewhat like a blade.

Unlike the topspin, it is not as necessary to tilt the racquet head during the motion of the slice, but there is a very slight flick of the racquet head required in order to get the necessary depth from the shot. However, the racquet head should be angled in the opposite direction to the topspin stroke. The best proponents of this shot are Roger Federer and Steffi Graf, so watching how they have executed it is particularly worthwhile.

Although the slice is a one-handed stroke in execution, the second hand can be placed on the throat of the racquet to help guide it during the initial take back. Bending your knees is particularly important for adopting a slice with a lower bouncing ball. The swing and follow-through is also different from the topspin groundstroke, with a smoother motion necessary. However, it is still important to accelerate through the ball when hitting a slice, rather than stabbing at the shot.

The weight transference is the same as with other groundstrokes, but it is probably slightly less dramatic. You can still hit a good slice off the back foot, which is sometimes necessary considering that it can often be used as a defensive option.

It is important to avoid chopping down on the ball, rather hitting through it with a longer swing. If you racquet moves down vertically then it will be harder to meet the ball in exactly the right spot. This results in too much cut and spin, and will make it difficult to make the ball travel through the court satisfactorily, with the necessary velocity. A rather limp slice shot will result.

Finally, the service is obviously a vital weapon for every single tennis player. Although it can be a difficult stroke to master at first, it is also the shot on the tennis court over which you have the most control, as it is effectively the same every single time. You don't have to deal with the ball coming back to either; you decide where the ball is placed.

This means that they serve is the answer to a tricky question often asked by coaches, namely which is the easiest stroke in tennis. While it is tempting and natural to say forehand, you're supposed to answer with serve, as it's the only stroke over which you have total control, and always involves exactly the same process.

Speaking of process, it is a good idea to have a set pattern leading up to your serve, similar to the way that golfers prepare their swings. You will notice that virtually all professional players have a specific process. The British player Jo Konta bounces the ball at almost head height, while Novak Djokovic is known for bouncing the ball an inordinate number of times. Boris Becker used to swing the racquet in an ostentatious fashion (a mannerism that I copied when building my own service process), while Ivan Lendl used to twitch the racquet head shortly before serving.

There are three basic types of serve - the flat, power serve, the slice serve, and the kick serve. You should certainly be able to hit the flat and slices serves from exactly the same ball toss, which should be a little out in front of you.

The power serve involves you closing the racquet head to a great extent, particularly when serving down the T.

Closing the racquet head minimizes the amount of spin on the ball, which means it will travel through the court with more velocity. With this serve, you are pretty much aiming to hit the ball with the absolute center of the racquet head.

However, for the angled power serve out wide, you should hit the ball just to the left of center of the racquet head (for right-handers), with a slightly tilted face. This results in the ball coming off the racquet head at an angle, forcing it towards the corner of the service box. You can serve out wide without tilting the racquet head, but this is considered a rather crude approach.

The slice serve involves a similar motion to the power serve, but the racquet head is angled in a more pronounced fashion in order to generate the spin required by this technique. The actual execution of the service doesn't really change, so we will deal with this next.

When hitting the service, it is important to take the racquet back as far as possible. You should also bend your elbow, much in the fashion of throwing a ball. Your upper arm should be practically at right angles to your lower arm, with the elbow ultimately acting like a catapult when you hit through the ball.

You should stretch as high as possible when serving, as mentioned previously. It is also really important to watch the ball extremely closely, as even world-class players can make a horrible hash of the service if they don't watch the ball carefully. The serve also involves the transference of weight from back foot to front foot that we have discussed with other strokes, but this process is more dramatic and explosive with the service motion.

If you get the ball toss right, then your momentum should carry you forwards once you have served, and you will inevitably find yourself inside the court markings. It is also important to aim downwards when serving, as if the ball toss and striking of the serve are executed correctly then the angle of service required will be somewhat less than perpendicular to the court.

The kick serve is the trickiest serve to master, and shouldn't really be attempted until you are confident with the basic service motion. The kick serve involves throwing the ball a little behind yourself, and bending your back with an unusual racquet motion, in order to generate a large amount of topspin, or 'kick'. The motion of the racquet head is much more like a topspin shot, with the strings brushing up against the back of the ball in order to generate the requisite spin.

This is one that will take many hours on the practice court in order to master.

Making the Right Decisions and Avoiding Tennis Mistakes

The early years of your tennis career shouldn't be seen as the be all and end all of your development. You still have plenty of time to recover from any damage done. But it will certainly make it a lot easier on you later on if you have the right approach to the game from day one.

Court positioning is absolutely critical to the game of tennis, and good players consistently take up excellent positions on the courts. One of the simplest tips that I can give you immediately is to ensure that you don't drift into no man's land. This is a common mistake by beginners, whereby they stand somewhere between the baseline and service line after serving, as the momentum of the service motion naturally takes them into this position.

It is essential after serving to either rush forwards with the intention of making a volley, or consciously make an effort to step back behind the baseline. Otherwise, you will end up getting caught in the middle of nowhere, particularly if your opponent makes a good standard return. It is surprising how many learners make this error, and I can remember coaching my friend in our school championships and noticing that he was doing precisely this. Correcting this simple mistake combined with a few other small pointers massively improved his game, and he was able to reach the semi-finals of the tournament.

Another major issue for young players in particular is whether or not to use two hands on the racquet. It is very common to use two hands when learning. I must say that when I first played short tennis, I had a two-handed forehand. Rafael Nadal had a two-handed forehand until he was about 10 years old. And a player I played with regularly, called James Fox, used two hands on both sides until the age of 12. And he later ran Greg Rusedski very close at the British Championships.

So there is nothing wrong with using two hands initially, while you learn at the game of tennis. But if you want to get better then you will simply have to switch to a one-handed forehand; I would recommend this at as young an age as possible. I know that I was told long before I actually played proper tennis that I had to use one hand on the forehand side. And I'm glad I tried this at a young age, as it made learning the technique far easier.

You simply won't be able to impart the level of spin required with two hands, and this will be a massive disadvantage for your forehand in the long run. So if you're anything other than a casual tennis player, you should certainly switch to a one-handed forehand by the time you are 10 years old. Ideally, you should begin with the correct technique, and only use one hand from day one.

Upgrading your equipment is a particular tricky subject in tennis, but this will become essential as your proficiency in the game develops. Knowing what equipment to buy can be a conundrum, but there is a relatively simple answer to this predicament. You should buy a new racquet when your current equipment is limiting your performance.

You should never change the way that you play tennis in order to suit your racquet. Rather, your equipment should suit your overall game. A good rule of thumb for younger players is that they should use the heaviest and most powerful racquet that they can swing comfortably without hurting their shoulders. However, it is important to note that some fatigue can result in the first few days of using a new racquet, so don't judge equipment too hastily. This should not persist in the longer term, as your body adjusts to the new racquet.

The reason for moving to a heavier racquet is that it will help you answer of the power of your opponents, as you move up the tennis ladder. Trust me, this will be absolutely essential as you attempt to return serve. You should also be wary of copying your particular heroes on the courts, especially if your game is radically different. For example, I have used Roger Federer's Wilson Pro Staff racquet, and it doesn't suit my game at all. I need more power from a racquet than his control-focused equipment delivers (in fact, he used to use a racquet with an even smaller head, which I find scarcely believable!).

The type of racquet that you use is a somewhat dependent on style as well. If you have an exaggerated backswing and follow through then you should definitely think about using a low-powered racquet with high control. Probably a stiffness rating in the region of 65 is advisable, with a beam around 20mm. The Wilson Pro Staff that I just mentioned is one such example of a racquet with these characteristics, with the Yonex Tour G310 being another good option.

Those players who hit with a high amount of topspin, and tend to loop the ball into the court, need more power in the strings. Bablolat, used by Rafael Nadal, would then become a manufacturer that you should definitely consider. Head is also known for delivering racquets with massive power spots, so its products also merit consideration.

As you get older and progress as a tennis player, the racquet head that you use will generally become smaller. However, this is also a delicate balance, as some of the larger head size racquets are heavier, and can thus be tricky for the youngest players to deal with.

Overall, the racquet head size that you utilize may look something like a parabola, beginning somewhere in the middle, reaching a peak in size as your body develops, and becoming smaller again as your strength delivers power on its own without the aid of the strings.

So by the time you have successfully implemented all of the advice in this chapter, you should be a rather proficient tennis player. Of course, this is easier said than done! But with consistent practice and a commitment to improvement, you can make steady gains that eventually result in real results on the tennis court.

Chapter 3 – Getting Serious, Getting Good

We're now reaching the stage of the book and your tennis development that will only be reached by those with either unusual levels of natural talent, a real passion for the sport of tennis, a determination to improve the standard of tennis that they play, or, ideally, a combination of the three.

If I am 100% honest, I only had two of these three qualities. I seemingly had a pretty good level of natural talent, and I hated losing and am naturally drawn towards competition. So I was able to reach the stage of being a good club and tournament tennis player pretty rapidly. However, in the long run I didn't have the passion for the sport of tennis that is required in order to be a professional. I just didn't enjoy competing the way that such obvious lovers of the game as Roger Federer, Rafael Nadal and Lleyton Hewitt do.

So before entering into this chapter, I believe it's important for everyone involved in tennis to ask themselves some serious questions. What do you want to get out of the game, and do you really enjoy tennis enough to invest the amount of time, effort and commitment required to make marginal gains as your play improves?

I ended up walking away from tennis in a serious capacity as I simply became bored of playing. I later picked up the game socially, and now playing regularly at my local club once more. But I don't play singles, and have absolutely no interest in competing.

This may sound like blasphemy, but the reason for this is that I played an enormous amount of tennis when I was younger. And the most important part of this is not the competing, not the matches, not the tournaments, but the practice and training. And trust me when I say that if you are not extremely passionate about tennis that this will get boring.

What you need to do to reach the highest levels of the game is repetitive. It involves thousands of hours of practice, of continuous drills that are not in and of themselves enjoyable. Some people find the results and outcome of those drills enjoyable, but practicing tennis isn't particularly fun, especially when you're not really tangibly improving any more. Imagine Nadal and Federer training day after day after day, and still trying to improve their games. This must be a rather difficult task!

So I would always say that the key aspect of any top class tennis player, or in fact anyone who achieves anything approaching mastery in any tricky discipline, is sheer love for what they're doing. It is that makes the pianist sit at their instrument for hours every day, which makes the chess grandmaster strive to study chess positions until they've memorized them, and which drove Rafael Nadal to train really hard to come back from injury even when he was already extremely wealthy and had won the French Open more times than anyone else in history.

If you don't have this drive and passion, it is phenomenally unlikely that you'll be successful in the game of tennis. So please bear this in mind before you go any further, and understand that concerted improvement will be impossible without this quality.

If, in the cold light of day, you do not possess it then you should concentrate on tennis as being a fun sport, a good way of keeping fit, and an enjoyable social activity.

This chapter will deal with the following:

- Whether you should play singles, doubles, or both;

- What equipment you should be using as you become proficient;

- The importance of the backhand, particularly at junior level;

- Whether you should have a one-handed or two-handed backhand;

- Balancing the importance of improvement versus getting results;

- Should you be coming to the net when you're still small in height.

Your Skillset, Your Aims and Choosing Singles and Doubles

Now that you have become somewhat technically proficient, you can begin to think about the aims of your tennis. Is this something that you are serious about, or rather a mild diversion in your life? What I would say is that you really need to show some talent in the game by your adolescence if you are to have any hope of pursuing it seriously. Tennis can still be enjoyed, even if you are a run-of-the-mill club player, but all strong players peak pretty early.

It is probably premature to begin specializing in your tennis career at this juncture. But already your development has definitely begun, and the reality is that you may not stray too far from these initial foundations. Already, the pattern of your play for years to come has probably been somewhat set, and it is certainly worthwhile to pay heed to your own particular idiosyncrasies.

There is no need for you to decide to be a doubles specialist or clay-court grinder while you are still a developing player, but it is definitely beneficial to understand one's own strengths and weaknesses. Do you exhibit a particularly good touch around the net? Do you relish long rallies? Are you able to hit with a lot of spin? Do you strike the ball with significantly greater power than your contemporaries? And do you have an intimidating serve?

While many players are late developers and bloomers, the answer to these questions will provide you with an imprint of your likely tennis direction. It is important to keep your options open and participate in varied tennis activity as you develop as a player. You will often find that your particular strengths are almost inured in nature, though, and that they become more magnified over time regardless of how you may train.

I should probably mention at this point that almost no-one sees him or herself as a doubles player! I know that when I played competitively I much preferred playing singles. However, in reality I was probably a better doubles player, and my skillset was probably more suited to this form of the game. Possibly if I had concentrated on doubles I could have gone on and played professionally.

Certainly, better players than me have switched to doubles and enjoyed significant success, perhaps most notably Andy Murray's brother Jamie. His former mixed doubles partner Martina Hingis is another player whose skillset was particularly particularly suited to the two-player variant of tennis. So you may fight kicking and screaming against the idea that you are a doubles specialist, but you can certainly bear this in mind as you observe your tennis qualities developing.

As you become a better player, you should also be using more advanced equipment. I would certainly say that by the time you reach double figures in age that you should be using full-sized racquets, and certainly play on a full-size court regularly. This may still feel challenging at this age, but all serious players that I have encountered had graduated on to the adult game by this time.

The Importance of the Backhand

As I mentioned in the previous chapter, the backhand is a particularly important stroke in your junior tennis armory. It really can make the difference between a decent junior and a successful contender. While the bankhand is undoubtedly a key stroke in tennis, the shot also requires the young player to make a major decision at a fairly early age.

Should you go two-handed, or should you opt for the classical one-handed backhand? Well, I will make two seemingly contradictory statements on this subject! But don't worry; I intend to explain myself fully!

Firstly, I absolutely prefer the one-handed backhand from an aesthetic perspective. It is the definitive way to play tennis, it simply looks beautiful, and such exponents as Roger Federer, Stanislas Wawrinka and Richard Gasquet have become appealing and popular players due to their one-handers.

Conversely, I would recommend all junior players to utilize a two-handed backhand. The only possible exception to this would be if they simply cannot get to grips with a two-hander. This shouldn't be considered too alarming, as this was literally the situation that Roger Federer found himself in as a young player. He just could not hit the ball competently with two hands on the backhand side, and thus opted for the wonderful one-handed backhand that he still uses today.

However, let's look at this in practical terms. Aside from Federer and Wawrinka, virtually every top player in the game today utilizes a two-handed backhand. At the time of writing, all of the top 10 players in the world apart from Federer have two-handers. And there are only three players in the top 32 in the world with one-handed backhands as well.

It isn't impossible to play at the highest level with one-hand, as Federer has emphatically proved, and as the young gun Denis Shapovalov is also demonstrating. But there is a reason why 80-90% of top players utilize a two-handed approach. You simply gain far more stability for the stroke with two hands, it just makes the whole swing considerably more solid and steady.

Hitting the ball with a one-handed backhand is extremely difficult. It might look easy when Federer is doing it, but I can assure you that it requires an extraordinary amount of technical ability. Certainly to hit through the ball with a one-hander is tremendously challenging. I couldn't do it with any consistent level of proficiency.

However, sliced backhands do require you to use one hand on the racquet, and this is an aspect of the backhand that you should definitely develop. But it is so much easier to hit a good slice with one hand than to hit a competent topspin backhand with the same setup. I could do the former easily, but never had the ability to hit a strong topspin one-handed backhand.

While I wouldn't necessarily see eye-to-eye with the famous tennis supremo Nick Bollettieri on every subject, it is notable that he has publicly advocated the two-hander as being superior. When commentating on Wimbledon, Bolletieri noted that the one-handed backhand is beautiful to watch, but that he would almost without exception recommend young players to utilize two hands.

This represents a sea change in coaching from when I played the game, as at that time the one-handed backhand was generally recommended by the LTA. But the equipment used in tennis, and ultimately the game itself, has changed so much since then that I believe that the two-handed backhand is almost obligatory.

Look at the long, grinding rallies played out by Novak Djokovic and Andy Murray in their epic Australian Open finals in particular. It is extremely difficult to maintain the level of consistency that these two great players exhibited with a one-handed backhand. This is why when Djokovic was beating Federer regularly he always targeted his backhand side, knowing that it was more likely to break down than his own two-hander.

By all means try playing the game with one hand on both groundstrokes, but I would certainly recommend all younger players to opt for a two-handed backhand at the first opportunity.

Net Play and the Value of Results vs Performance

We haven't discussed volleying much as of yet, so I wanted to devote a section to the subject of net play. In my opinion, this is the hardest part of the game, particularly for younger players. Indeed, many professionals arrive on the ATP Tour nowadays with a pretty minimal net game. Even some of the very best players in the world.

But it is clearly preferable to be at least somewhat proficient at volleying, as it is such a good way to finish off points. You can certainly do the majority of your work on a tennis court from the baseline, but you'll be something short of a complete player without the confidence to come to the net. Even someone like Nadal, who patently didn't initially relish net play considering that he plays doubles entirely from the back of the court, has worked tirelessly to improve his net game, and is now one of the most capable volleyers in the game.

Nonetheless, it is tough for kids to commit to coming to the net, as they can so easily be lobbed. This is where you have to to consider the importance of performance versus results. I can remember coming off court after one victory as a younger player, and expecting my coach to be pleased. But he instead dismissed my performance as 'hacking' (often described now as pushing).

In short, I was playing conservatively, instead of approaching the game in the right way. This is an important lesson to learn, as results aren't everything, particularly when you're learning the game. It's important to get into good habits and a healthy approach to tennis, rather than being too focused on the outcome. Process not outcomes; it's a mantra that all people who excel in their sports subscribe to.

I have included some drills later in the book to encourage volleying to develop. But I also think young players should make an attempt to come to the net during matches, as this is the best way to learn, and there is more to volleying than simply hitting the ball. Anticipating what your opponent will do is also key to net play, and there is no substitute for match play in developing this technique.

Yes, you will get lobbed sometimes. Yes, it can be a little frustrating at times. But if it's hard at first, it will also get a lot easier later on, as you grow into your body. And by then you will have established some of the techniques that will hold you in good stead as you become a more advanced tennis player. Never shy away from any aspect of the game if you want to reach your true potential. If you're completely focused on results then you run the risk of becoming, in modern parlance, a pusher, which will not get you anywhere if you want to be a serious tennis player.

Conversely, if you only want to play a competent game of tennis in a social setting then you can ignore this advice! But even a lot of social tennis is doubles. And this requires volleying. So there really is no excuse to avoid the net like the plague.

Once you have learned the skills discussed in this chapter, you are well on your way to becoming a strong player. Indeed, I would argue that any junior player with a reliable backhand will almost inevitably be extremely strong. In the next chapter, we will discuss getting into the mainline tennis system.

Chapter 4 – Getting Into the System

If you persevere and become an accomplished tennis player then at some point you were going to think seriously about the potential of playing the game professionally. Almost everyone does who ever plays tennis at county level. If you're good enough to reach that standard then you must have a reasonable level of ability, and you must have invested a significant amount of time in playing the game competitively. People of this nature naturally want to take the next step, yet few are successful in realizing their ambitions and dreams.

Central to your success or otherwise will be gaining recognition from official bodies that oversee the game in your country. Please note that you don't necessarily have to to follow the well-trodden official path; you can certainly plow an independent furrow in the game of tennis. However, I would struggle to point to any successful tennis player who hasn't established himself or herself as a formidable junior at a young age, and delivered some outstanding results in official tournaments.

Above all else, it's really important to come into contact with other outstanding players as quickly as possible, once it is established that you have potential. Your tennis will stall if you don't play against the best of the best, and learn from playing against people at the same level, and even higher levels than you. Indeed, one of the most valuable things you can do as a junior is enter tournaments featuring older players; you will learn more from this challenge than by beating lesser individuals.

So this chapter will outline how you can achieve the official recognition that will enable you to develop your career, and how best to deliver and showcase the skillset required to achieve this. These topics will be discussed:

- What makes a talented and genuinely promising junior;

- What do you need to develop in order to achieve this;

- What drills should you be doing at this time;

- What fitness program should you be following;

- Should you be trying to get into the system anyway;

- What most benefits a proficient and somewhat strong junior player.

What Makes a Top Junior Tennis Player?

I will discuss my ideas and observations regarding what makes a top junior player shortly, but it is first valuable to draw on the research of Piotr Unierzyski of the University of Physical Education in Poznan, Poland. Unierzyski examined talented young tennis players over an eight-year period at the turn of the century, and discovered that there are certain patterns among these gifted individuals that can be recognised.

The first of his observations, that these players were around four months younger than the mean age for the group, seems to be a statistical anomaly. However, it is notable that they were slimmer than the average 12-13 year-old tennis players. I would certainly agree with this assessment and observation, as I believe that a mild ectomorph build tends to be the best somatotype for tennis. To briefly explain this, somatotypes are essentially different body types, and the ectomorph stature is lean, tall and slim.

While other sporting pursuits benefit from a muscular frame, it is certainly better to be lean, flexible and wiry to play tennis. Top-heavy professional tennis players, such as Mark Philippoussis, have almost inevitably experienced knee problems, with the legendary Rafael Nadal having reportedly slimmed down significantly in order to counteract this.

When one thinks of the likes of Novak Djokovic and Andy Murray, wiry is definitely a word that comes to mind. This doesn't mean that you can't play decent tennis if you're a big built guy, but you may not be participating in the sport that is your genetic match. I must say that my body tends towards ectomorphic, and although I played virtually every ballgame for my school, including soccer, cricket and rugby, I was always best at tennis by some distance.

The researcher also discovered that the talented players began their tennis education at a mean average of six years-old. But, in accordance with what I recommended previously, they had begun playing in tournaments at an average age of nine. They even played less singles and doubles matches per year on average, underlining the importance of practice and development rather than excessive competition at this age.

Unierzyski also found that these players were doing two hours extra fitness training per week compared to the average tennis player, and that the talented individuals also benefited from strong support from their parents. However, Dr. Piotr also noted that the parents were involved in the development of their children, but not to an excessive degree. They were supportive without being pushy.

Finally, the most important point, in my opinion at least, is that the talented players were noticeably less powerful than their contemporaries. This may seem like a complete anomaly, but in my opinion it is extremely significant.

Many young players excel, in results terms at least, when playing in junior tennis by massively overpowering their opponents. This looks impressive when there is a gulf in strength, but this inevitably narrows over time, and it is at this later adolescent age that the cream tends to rise to the top. Boris Becker often states that he wasn't an outstanding player when was younger, but he rapidly blossomed into the youngest ever winner of the Wimbledon singles title.

Relying on strength and physical power can, in fact, result in a player developing bad habits. And then, when the gap in power begins to diminish, it can be almost impossible to reverse these bad habits and learn new tricks, as one's technique and whole approach to the game has been set in stone.

That is why it is essential to hit the ball the right way from day one, and to practice the appropriate techniques and general approach to the game. This will pay dividends in the longer term, even if the immediate results in matches may not be as impressive. Power can dominate junior tennis, but it can also give a completely false impression of the ability of an individual. More valuable is to develop a well-rounded game, which will mature much more favorably at a later date.

A great junior tennis player shows an aptitude for all of the strokes, is reluctant to favor a particular strength or cherished part of his or her game, and moves ably around the court, with a good deal of awareness and court craft. Equally, the skilled junior is not afraid to go for his or her shots, and looks to hit winners when the opportunity arises, rather than simply putting the ball back into court and interminably waiting for a mistake from an opponent.

These skills will be noticeable completely regardless of results. Every successful junior that I have ever observed had these characteristics from a young age, and was willing to enable them to develop, even if it meant falling behind contemporaries occasionally in terms of tournament wins.

There are two simple drills that I would particularly advocate in order to develop these skills. And they can be easily summarized as simply developing side-to-side and front-to-back proficiency.

The first drill is the one that you will regularly see professional players utilizing. Stand a couple of feet behind the baseline, in a flexible position that is neither excessively attacking nor defensive. And then have a ball machine, or competent human feeder, push you from one side of the base line to the other, back and forth, back and forth, while you attempt to retrieve and hit as many balls as quickly and accurately as possible. This should be a baseline grind, a real high-intensity workout, which helps you develop the quality and stamina required to hang tough from the back of the court.

I would also advocate while doing this to remain the same distance from the baseline at all times. This makes it much harder, and is reflective of the court positioning of someone like Federer, who always attempts to maintain a stake on the baseline. Of course, there are other ways of playing the game, with Nadal often treating miles behind the baseline with great effectiveness. But I think in the early days of development it is better to give yourself less time to play strokes, so you become accustomed to the ball arriving at your racquet with pace.

The other drill does require human assistance, but it is a fun one to do. Begin at the back of the court with a groundstroke, which you will return straight to a human player standing close to the net. Then follow in your groundstroke immediately, and hit a half volley on the way to the net. Then make a third shot of a volley, aiming the ball straight back to your human feeder. He or she will then lob you, and you should chase this ball back and try to return it right back to your opponent. Then begin the drill again from the back of the court. Repeat this over and over and over again.

Both of these repetitions will enable you to practice and develop two of the key skills in the game of tennis. Your ultimate success will be largely defined by your ability to produce consistent groundstrokes while travelling from side-to-side, and equally your competence at moving back and forth from the front to the back of the court while playing a variety of different strokes from various positions.

Drill these two skills with regularity and seriousness, and you are well on your way to becoming a proper tennis player.

The Work Required to be a Top Junior

Discipline is the key quality required to the successful in tennis at any age. And this means that any child who chooses the sport must feel an almost undying passion for playing it. There has to be an enduring fascination with the game of tennis in order to go through all of the drills and fitness routines required to become capable.

It's not enough to practice and train, you must engage with training and practice in the appropriate fashion. This can be extremely difficult for children in particular, as emotions naturally play a big role in their overall behavior. It can also be difficult to balance the demands of education with the level of practice and training required to play top junior tennis.

I know that I struggled with this, as I didn't enjoy school, and often didn't feel in the right frame of mind to engage in repetitive, mentally and physically draining tennis practice after a day at school. I find it nothing short of amazing that the very top players can keep dragging themselves into the gym or on to the practice court. But they are special people, and profoundly love the game of tennis.

And that's what it takes to get to the top. And this is why I believe that passion for the sport is absolutely the most important aspect of playing tennis at a high-level. If you don't possess this passion then you simply won't want to do what is required to maximize your talent.

Equally, this is why I believe pushing your child to attempt to play any sport professionally is pointless. If they don't really, really want to do it then they will get fed up with playing eventually, and possibly even come to resent their parents' 'encouragement'. If there is one thing children are good at, particularly adolescents, it is rebelling against their parents!

Another thing to bear in mind is that young players can develop at completely different rates. Genetics, size, emotional and psychological maturity, and other factors can all play a role, and just because someone is particularly good at the age of 12, it doesn't mean that they will later be world-class at 21. Indeed, many young players are later overtaken by players who were less talented at a younger age. Development is unpredictable, which is another reason that you shouldn't concentrate on results too much at a young age, and should instead prioritize building the fundamentals of a solid tennis game.

Nonetheless, it is absolutely advisable to introduce your child to tennis at as young an age as possible. I didn't play on a proper tennis court until the age of eight, but I had already won the county and North Midlands region short tennis titles by this time, as well as participating in the British Championships. I had a fairly meteoric rise to this level, though, as I competed in the British finals just six months after playing a shot tennis competitively for the first time.

However, thinking back to my childhood, I spent a great deal of time in the back garden playing sport. I definitely played a fair bit of informal tennis, along with cricket and soccer. So I really believe that I had already formed some of the hand-eye coordination and basic techniques required by the time I began to play competitively, and this probably partly explains why I was instantly the best player in my school by a country mile.

Thus, the ideal age to start playing tennis is around 3 or 4. Don't underestimate the value of introducing your child to a bat and ball at this age. Of course, they don't need to be on a full-size court at this tender age, and they certainly shouldn't be using full-site equipment, or playing competitively. But by all means introduce your children to sport, and tennis, at this age, and show them how much fun at the game can be. Something may resonate with them, and all future champions began from these humble beginnings.

Be supportive towards your child, and nurture their potential, rather than living vicariously through them. The BBC recently ran an item on Ray Wood, a 38 year-old who grew up in the city of Liverpool. By his own admission, he is trying to "create two of the greatest female tennis players the planet has ever seen". This isn't a laudable ambition, it is laughable.

Great champions cannot be created through desire and practice alone, if that were possible then we would all be winning Wimbledon! It is inordinately tough to make it to the very top, and this should never be set as a goal, let alone from a young age. Indeed, the father of the Williams sisters, Richard Williams, emphasized the importance of ensuring that children know there is a big, wide world outside of the tennis court.

"Tennis is just a game. I'm not proud of what my daughters have done in tennis. I'm proud of my daughters for who they are, and for what they've achieved outside tennis," Williams commented.

It is also wise to separate parenting and coaching, otherwise your children will get sick of seeing you!

Playing professional-standard tennis is a labour of love. It is thousands of hours of repetitive practice, which can only be undertaken by someone truly in love with the game of tennis. You can put that opportunity in front of a young person, but you cannot force them to walk through that particular door. Furthermore, you have to accept that every player has a genetic limit, and you cannot push anyone beyond this, no matter how hard you try. But more on that later.

Do You Need to be in the Tennis System to Succeed?

Having your child at a major academy has become a status symbol. But it's certainly not necessary to go down this route in order to be successful. However, I think there is one aspect of a tennis education that is essential if a player is to reach his or her potential. You need to play against strong players, and you need to be beaten and outplayed by better, more skilled players.

Everyone I have encountered who made it into the professional game trained with particularly talented young players from a very early age. I know that I began playing on county squads from the age of nine, which is only a few months after I had initially began playing proper tennis.

This is another important point to note. The acceptance of a young player into the system is really a barometer of overall talent. When I played at a decent standard, there were around 20-30 players of my age in the elite county system in the LTA region in which I grew up. Bear in mind that there are 48 ceremonial counties in Britain, meaning that there are around 1,000 players of your age group within the LTA system at any time.

That is just one age group within one country, and you should further bear in mind that players who have won junior grand slams, and been ranked world number 1, have struggled to succeed on the professional tour. If you're not good enough to get into the system from a fairly young age, and play county / state standard tennis with other promising young players, you're not going to be able to play professional tennis. You can certainly improve as a tennis player, and eventually become a strong club player, but some ability needs to manifest itself from a fairly young age if you're to have the genetic potential to become part of the elite. And when I say 'elite', I mean top 250 in the world, not Wimbledon winner.

These are the most important aspects of getting into the system; having your level of ability effectively rubber-stamped, and gaining access to a wide variety of players at your level. I am sceptical that professional coaching is particularly beneficial once you reach a certain age.

Really, by the age of nine or 10, you have already learnt how to hit the tennis ball, and will make extremely limited technical adjustments for the remainder of your career. It is very unusual to get a player such as Nadal, who made fundamental changes to his technique at around the age of 10. But one can also say that the change that he made, switching from one hand to two hands, is the most common major technical switch.

Putting in the hours on the practice court, with the odd word of input and encouragement from an experienced coach, is really what is required to develop as a player. To some extent, I believe that academies are really stealing a living, making completely false promises to people of modest natural ability.

While I personally believe that any one of modest natural ability can become a proficient tennis player with determination and commitment, there is a massive difference between this and becoming a tennis champion. Yet I would bet my bottom dollar that the overwhelming majority of parents who put their kids into these academies hope that they will blossom into some incredible ATP or WTA champion.

The odds of this are extremely slim. And it doesn't matter how much money you spend on coaching, or what quality of players your child comes into contact with, there is no magic wand that can be waved, no elixir they can drink that will make them into a champion if they don't have it in their body. But you'd better believe that the academy will take your money completely regardless of the level of ability of your child.

We will examine academies further still in the next chapter. But if your child can't make it on his or her own, you really should ask yourself the question of whether they are likely to make it in an extremely competitive environment, against potentially some of the best young players in the world, and also whether their education wouldn't be better served elsewhere.

Chapter 5 – Surviving in the System

Getting in the system is one thing. Surviving and prospering in the system is entirely another. There are plenty of people ready to exploit the sincere intentions of both young tennis players and their parents. Equally, many parents think they know better than seasoned and experience professional coaches. There is definitely a balance to be struck here, but it is important for you to understand some of the problems that young players typically encounter.

There is nothing more flattering to the young tennis player than being offered an opportunity to train with prestigious coaches, or even in some of the world's most well-known academies. And this can undoubtedly represent a superb opportunity. But you won't get the most out of this experience if you don't approach it in the right manner, and for some people it is, quite frankly, a complete waste of time regardless of their approach.

Furthermore, some young people will thrive better outside of the academy and professional environment, at least at a young and tender age. There is also a balance to be struck between developing as a tennis player and as a human being. There is no doubt that the latter is considerably more important than the former, and getting this delicate balance right at a young age is critical for every young person.

Meanwhile, you're now in a position where you need to make serious decisions about your tennis, and the direction that it will go in the future. While the games and improvements that you will make at this time will be smaller than earlier in your developmental cycle, it is these few percentage points that really separate the good players from the very good and professional class performers.

With this in mind, this chapter will address the following topics:

- How to avoid some of the pitfalls that professional coaches will put before you;

- The dichotomy / debate between commitment, discipline and leading a balanced life as a child;

- What do the top coaches, talent spotters and official programs look for in a young player;

- What is the difference between a good and very good player, and what should you do to become very good;

- Should you specialize in playing on a certain surface;

- Should you be playing singles, doubles, or both at this time;

Dealing with Big Academies

Attending a tennis academy is all the rage nowadays, particularly for anyone with a modicum of talent. Several high-profile academies have sprung up all over the world, making lofty promises regarding what they offer young people and tennis players. Attending such an academy can almost be a badge of honour for certain individuals within the upper middle classes, but does attending such an institution makes sense, and is it really necessary?

It is interesting to note that the legendary Rafael Nadal has been involved in setting up an academy on his native Spanish island of Mallorca. I cannot help being slightly sceptical about this initiative, inevitably viewing it as more of a cash grab from a wealthy individual rather than something that is absolutely necessary.

Obviously, Nadal's name on any academy will be an outstanding selling point, but it's not as if attendees of the Rafael Nadal Academy get to tuck into breakfast with him on a daily basis! The Spanish left-hander is far too busy participating in his extremely successful tennis career to worry too much about daily involvement in any tennis academy.

It is also worth noting that Nadal and his family decided against enrolling Rafael in a tennis academy when he was younger. His coach and uncle Toni Nadal specifically stated that the family considered it completely unnecessary to move to America in order to pursue his tennis career, stating that such activity could easily take place at home.

While the Nadal family may argue that this academy provides an opportunity for young people living in Spain, there is no doubt that it will remain outside of the price range of most young tennis players. Costing €56,000 euros annually, the Rafael Nadal Academy is simply outside of the price range of all but the elite. Not all of this figure relates to tennis activities, and it is claimed that attendees will also receive a top education. But I would seriously question the value of such an investment.

Other academies include the infamous IMG Bolletieri academy, and the recently opened Mouratoglou Tennis Academy in Nice, France. Again, only the upper, upper middle classes will ever be able to attend these academies with their own finance, which wrongly cements the idea that tennis is, and should be, an elitist sport.

Ultimately, very few people who attend these academies will come remotely close to playing at a professional standard, as it is not spending a large amount of money, or attending academies, which will ultimately decide this. In fact, such academies absolutely rely on hundreds of the players that are nowhere near good enough to progress to the professional game, otherwise they simply will not have a business model.

There are plenty of tales of young players at some of these academies being placed with lesser coaches, while the handful of really talented young players get the exclusive attention of the top teachers. After all, it's essential for them to be able to boast about the top players that they have 'created'. Why waste time and resources on coaching players who will never achieve this, when no one is ever going to hear about them anyway, and such young players certainly can't be used as a promotional gambit?

Rest assured, it doesn't matter whose name is on the can, such academies will be more than happy to take your money, while knowing all along about your son or daughter will never be anything approaching a professional tennis player.

The one thing that these academies do potentially offer, which I believe to be absolutely the most important aspect of your development as a young tennis player, is access to quality opposition. You will only learn and develop by playing against people who are better than you. But there are other ways to achieve this other than attending some institution which costs annually around double the average salary in the Western world.

The British Lawn Tennis Association estimates that developing a player from the age of 5 to 18 can cost around £250,000 ($300,000). Well, you can burn this entire figure in around five years at some of the most prestigious academies, underlining just how expensive they are. And I would be extremely careful about wishy-washy claims about the level of academic education that you will receive at such institutions; ultimately it is highly unlikely that they will be as good as private schools that cost significantly less.

If your child has real talent then the tennis playing authorities in your country will want them on board. They are, after all, tasked with creating champions. My advice would always be to deliver the best results possible in your early adolescent years, and then to approach the authorities for sponsorship and support.

If your son or daughter is good enough, it will definitely be forthcoming. If it isn't forthcoming then you should really ask yourself whether you are willing to fritter money away on an exorbitant tennis academy, when the key aspects of the game can be learned elsewhere, and your child will have an extremely minimal chance of success anyway. At the Nadal academy, you will pay €20,000 per year for food and accommodation. We can safely say that Rafa's not going to go hungry any time soon! But is it really worth it for your child?

There are rare examples of players from a modest background attending such academies and genuinely benefiting. For example, Andy Murray spent time in Spain, with his family having raised £40,000 in order for this to take place. But Murray had already won the Orange Bowl junior tournament by this time, with his brother having lost in the final. Clearly there was nothing too much wrong with their development up to this point, so I would strongly recommend any young player concentrating on achieving similar results, before worrying about academies.

Furthermore, it is my experience that professional coaches will hardly ever tell parents that their son or daughter isn't good enough. I have met a fewer scrupulous individuals who will do this, but for the most part they simply see dollar signs in front of their eyes, and are perfectly willing to allow parents to invest vast sums of money in what is essentially a black hole.

Don't kid yourself. Be honest about the talents, or otherwise, of your offspring.

Specializing or Keeping Your Options Open

One of the interesting aspects of tennis is its multi-surfaced nature. If you play soccer or American football, the condition of the pitch never really comes into consideration. But with tennis being played on significantly differing hard courts, indoors and outdoors, in searing heat and humidity, occasionally under dreary cloud cover (mostly in my native Britain!), quite often on carpet, although less so in the professional game, clay, grass, fast conditions, slow conditions, medium-paced conditions, low bouncing, high bouncing, and everything in between...there is a huge amount of variety in conditions.

This means that many players come to specialize in playing on a certain surface, although this tendency has diminished slightly in the modern era, as playing conditions have become somewhat more generic. Equally, with the singles and doubles games both being a viable part of the professional game, some players decide to specialize in one or another at a fairly young age.

The first thing to say is that this decision certainly doesn't need to be made in early adolescence. Virtually all strong tennis players participate in both singles and doubles right up until college, and will probably only decide to specialize in one or another when turning professional. Doubles can also teach skills that are useful on the singles court, which is a compelling reason to play as much doubles as possible when you are a young player.

By the time that you're a teenager, you will probably have established which one of the surfaces suits your game best. Equally, the surface that you grow up playing on the most will probably have a big impact on your development. It is no coincidence that Spain produces so many skilled clay courters, when there are a huge number of these courts in the sun-baked nation.

Nonetheless, I wouldn't recommend specializing in playing on a certain surface, possibly ever. Certainly it isn't something you should consider until you are a professional-standard player. Even if you reach that level you will need to play on all of the surfaces to a reasonably proficient level, so you might as well work hard on your game in all possible conditions, even if some of them are a bit of a grind.

From my personal experience, it is particularly important to gain a good balance between playing indoors and outdoors. I much preferred playing indoors, for several reasons, not least the fact that it is simply easier. There is no wind, rain, sunshine, or other distractions to influence the outcome of the game; essentially playing tennis indoors is pure tennis.

But as the majority of tournaments in your life will be outdoors, it is important to learn to deal with these things. You can't just throw your toys out of the pram if you turn up and the wind is blowing gustily. Great players adapt to their surroundings, and this is something that you should learn to do from a young age.

It is also important to get a feel for the impact of weather conditions on your body. One thing that I know I would have found particularly difficult would be playing in hotter conditions. This was rarely an issue in the United Kingdom, but I do remember one match in oppressive conditions during which I vomited at the side of the court. I was glad to come through that one after three and a half hours, having been told to play a tie-break by the organisers of the tournament at 11-all in the final set.

This is the sort of experience that you have to go through if you have any pretension of becoming a serious tennis player. Tennis isn't just about hitting the ball, it is about pushing your body to the limits of its capabilities. Watch the likes of Nadal, Djokovic and Murray in the professional game, and you will see what is required physically in order to excel in tennis. You can't reach this level without pushing yourself from a young age.

Concentrating on Tennis or Leading a Balanced Life

There is something of a dichotomy in the development of a young tennis player. On the one hand, reaching your potential in tennis requires a huge amount of commitment and discipline. Conversely, it is also important to lead a balanced life as a child, even if you are becoming serious about your tennis career.

I know that when I was in the LTA scheme, I was always advised to play other sports, and generally try to lead as enjoyable a life as possible. And I do think this is the correct approach to tennis. You need to take practice extremely seriously, even from a young age, but it should be about quality rather than quantity.

Martina Navratilova noted that she only played tennis for four hours per week while she was growing up. I probably played between 10 and 15 hours per week as a teenager, with maybe another 5 hours of physical training. Looking back, I believe that the amount I played was too much, but other players may thrive with that sort of workload.

But it's important to keep the emphasis on enjoyment. Tennis should never become a chore, as if it ever represents this then your chances of competing are zero. Look at Bernard Tomic in the professional game, he has quite obviously fallen out of love with playing tennis, and has been widely condemned for this. While I can understand this reaction, I can equally appreciate how he feels.

Tomic has spent thousands of hours on a tennis court from a young age, and has probably hit millions of tennis strokes by now. He is probably sick and tired of playing tennis, particularly as the professional circuit is such a grind. Yes, he is fortunate to be wealthy at a young age, and, yes, many people would swap places with him. But if you simply don't enjoy something, it is impossible to kid yourself that you actually do enjoy it.

And I believe that this enjoyment is absolutely central to every successful tennis player. You have to be unbelievably passionate about tennis to keep on the treadmill required to play at the highest level. That passion can only come from enjoyment of the game, which is why it is important for this to remain the emphasis of your tennis throughout your development.

Chapter 6 – Is Coaching Critical for Playing Professional-Standard Tennis?

In recent years, there has been something of a debate and public discourse regarding the way that young tennis players are raised. And this has been presented by the media as a dichotomy between those that flourish within the system, due to their own innate talents, and those who are raised by sometimes highly competitive and driven parents, with a master plan to make their offspring successful.

While this is a pleasing contradiction in terms, the reality is a bit more nuanced and complicated. Very few players can reach the professional game without the support of professional-standard coaching. Equally, it is certainly possible to succeed while retaining independence, and it's not necessarily essential to rely on the tried and tested route of receiving assistance from the tennis authorities in your country, allied to some of its approved and highly regarded coaches.

Although there is quite a bit to know about the game of tennis, it is also important to remember something fundamental at this point. This is a simple game! You do not need to overcomplicate what you're doing on a tennis court, and sometimes the level of analysis that takes place is unnecessary. Furthermore, you don't necessarily need to be a brilliant tennis player in order to make simple and valuable observations about the game of tennis.

For example, here is one observation that you probably haven't heard stated on television, at least not in these simple terms. Rafael Nadal is generally regarded as the greatest clay-court player of all-time. Do you know why? Because it's extremely difficult to hit the ball past him! On clay, Rafa takes this fundamental aim of the game almost out of the equation, meaning that every single match becomes a demoralizing war of attrition.

And the person most responsible for assisting Natal with developing this style of play has barely even played tennis. Toni Nadal can hardly play to club standard, and yet has been instrumental in the coaching of one of the greatest players of all-time.

It is too simplistic to say that Nadal has operated entirely outside of the Spanish system, though, and this is why the simple dichotomy often presented by the media is misleading. But you should also be clear that coaching tennis can be done with flair and success by those with less ability to play the game itself.

Thus, this chapter will address the following:

- Why numerous champions have been coached successfully by non-players;

- Why great players don't necessarily make great coaches;

- Why strategy isn't that important when you're a junior;

- Should you push your kids, or have a laissez-faire attitude;

Why Coaches Don't Need to be Great Players

Tennis is much like any other sport in many ways, not least the fact that ex-professionals often go on to be involved with the game once they have finished playing. This seems like a perfectly natural progression in their careers, and can often be extremely successful. But tennis is also somewhat different in that some of the most high profile individuals have not been coaches by particularly proficient tennis players.

This would seem odd in what is often considered to be a particularly technical sport. But there is a reason that it is possible to coach successfully without being a great player yourself. Tennis isn't complicated! This is not a complex or difficult game to understand, and once you have the basic techniques then the actual technical input required from coaches is pretty minimal.

If you don't believe me then check out the leaked notes that Andy Murray once left in a locker room. There is nothing earth-shattering, or even remotely interesting, about what is written on this paper. These are observations that could be made by almost anyone. Yet this is guidance that one of the very best tennis players in the world is utilizing. It should be clear from this that anyone with intelligence and a little vision is capable of coaching tennis, and even conceivably one of the very greatest players on the planet.

Of course, getting an opportunity like this is far from easy, but often everyday individuals are better at coaching tennis than even world-class players. Great players often don't make particularly effective coaches, as they demand too much perfection. It can be very difficult to teach something that you're extremely good at yourself, as you judge other people by your exalted standards.

Another issue is undoubtedly ego. The highly successful female tennis player Martina Hingis was once described as living in a golden cage. Tennis players are undoubtedly spoiled, and considering the material wealth and accolades that they actively receive, it is perhaps not surprising that some of them turn out to have a rather high opinion of themselves. This often doesn't translate into patience, or being a particularly skilled communicator.

Another problem with great players becoming great coaches is the assumption that because they can hit the ball really well they will be able to teach someone else to do the same. The reality is that no one can teach you how to hit a tennis ball. Some very minor guidance can be provided, but the only way you can make significant strides in tennis is by repetition and practice.

You have to be self-motivated and independent in order to succeed at tennis, and coaches should really foster this mentality rather than telling you what to do. It is then perhaps not surprising that some of the most successful coaches have been respected blood relations rather than outstanding tennis professionals.

Professional coaching can certainly be valuable. But at every level of the game, the most successful coaches are inevitably those who address what is between the ears of a player, and provoke a strong reaction from them.

Ultimately, by the age of 12 there are very few technical adjustments required, if you have been playing the game for the best part of a decade. Certainly, my coaches always concentrated on the mental aspect of the game, rather than trying to teach me how to hit the ball. I had already learnt this by the age of 12, and your child will have done so as well, if they have been practising for the best part of 10 years and have any talent whatsoever.

Why Strategy Isn't as Important For Young Tennis Players

Tactics and strategy always play a role in the game of tennis, but, in my opinion, they should be considered far less important at a younger age. The most important thing as you are developing is to ensure that you approach the game in the proper manner, and practice your strengths in a competitive scenario. While it is tempting to rely on strategy and tactics, this could be something of a mistake for the junior tennis player.

The reason for this is that many of your opponents will have quite obvious weaknesses at this tender age, and exploiting these may not be the best thing for your tennis development. Many young players also have physical deficiencies, which means that they cannot execute every aspect of the game as they might wish.

This is why being brilliant at the age of 12 doesn't necessarily translate into a sterling professional career. It is quite frequent for the best players at this age to be bigger and stronger than everyone else. And then, as everyone's bodies develop, the physical gap closes, and suddenly these once great players don't look so great any more.

Focusing on the weaknesses of your opponents, and indeed shying away from the weaker parts of your game, may get results in the shorter term, but you'll simply stall in your development as a player. You really need to improve the weaker parts of your game, and develop the ability to execute any stroke to any part of the court, while in a pressurised match situation.

When I played tennis competitively, my backhand was initially a major weakness. In order to become a more holistic player, I spent hours honing my backhand, and attempted to use it as much as possible in matches. It would have been much easier to run around my backhand and hit a large number of forehands, but this wouldn't have benefited my tennis development.

Putting results on the board at a young age can help build confidence, but it can also give you a completely false impression of where your game is actually at. So you should absolutely bear this in mind when playing competitively at a young age, or if you are the parent of a talented child.

Why You Shouldn't Push Your Kids

When I played tennis competitively, I witnessed many examples of parents pushing their children to play tennis, and even being rather hard on them when they perceived that they hadn't performed up to standard. Thankfully, my parents were absolutely brilliant in this regard, and never pushed me whatsoever.

Interestingly, none of the kids whose parents often behaved towards them in this way - that even at a young age I could recognize as being completely inappropriate - ever became professional tennis players. So all the emotion and difficulties that those people went through was ultimately futile. The children would probably have developed into better players if they had been left to their own devices. All the parents have really succeeded in doing is potentially damaging their relationships with their children.

Loving the game of tennis will be the number one factor in success, and it is hard to imagine that this love will develop if a child feels forced, or even coerced.

Another thing to bear in mind is that playing in tournaments at a young age isn't always beneficial. This does depend on the context, and I'm not saying that your child should never play in tournaments. But playing in youth tournaments can necessitate a great deal of travelling around, which can be both expensive and time-consuming. And then your child can lose in the first round!

Admittedly, many junior tournaments feature round robin groups to avoid this eventuality, and also a plate competition, for those who lose their first round matches. But you should still ask yourself whether travelling to tournaments, and playing matches in tournaments, is always the best usage of your time. Sometimes you can get match practice outside of a tournament context which is both more logistically convenient, and even of better quality.

It is nice to rack up some early tournament wins, and I know that when I was younger I was very proud of the trophies that I won. But they shouldn't be a massive badge of honor for a young player; the emphasis should always be on developing skills, and improving overall play.

Chapter 7 – The Importance of Talent vs The Value of Practice

Another discussion which has raged in the sporting world over the last few years is the debate regarding the importance of talent and practice. How far can you expect to go with minimal talent? And to what degree can practice take you to the very top?

This has always been a difficult question to answer, not least because it is difficult to define precisely what constitutes talent. Everyone who has played the game to a world-class level would be assumed to have a good degree of natural talent, yet all of them have also worked incredibly hard. It is clear that you cannot achieve success without both hard work and talent, but what level can you reach without any natural aptitude?

With this in mind, this chapter will address the importance of talent and the importance of practice, and discuss how far you can expect to go with minimal talent, looking at some of the examples from the professional game. It will also discuss some of the pitfalls for particularly talented players, and what players with relatively modest natural talent can do to negate this obstacle.

One of the primary debaters in this particular field has been the British journalist Matthew Syed. His book 'Bounce: The Myth of Talent and the Power of Practice' strongly and convincingly argues that practice is considerably more important than natural talent. This text makes the by now infamous assertion that mastery in any particular field requires 10,000 hours of sustained practice.

I might add to this that the nature of this practice is also extremely important. Half-hearted or inadequate practice will achieve very little. It is not practice that makes perfect, but rather perfect practice that makes perfect.

Can You Succeed in Tennis Without Talent?

One of the big questions that everyone wants answered in sport is to what degree are champions made, and to what degree are they born? This is a phenomenally difficult question to answer, and it may certainly differ from sport to sport. But I believe that there is a clear answer in the game of tennis at least.

Before I get on to this subject, I want to emphasize my belief that anyone with the physical capability to get out on a tennis court and play tennis has the potential to reach a decent level of proficiency. This is far from easy. It does require a huge amount of determination and practice, particularly as your games begin to plateau. At a certain point, you will stop making rapid progress, and begin to make very marginal gains, if any whatsoever.

However, there is an inspiring video on YouTube which illustrates the sort of competence that can be achieved with sheer bloody-minded perseverance. It is entitled "Guy Plays Table Tennis Every Day for a Year". The video in question features a rather talentless table tennis player. At the start of the video we see that he is barely able to hit the ball on to a table tennis table. The video then depicts him practising the game for at least one hour a day, every day, for one year. By the end of that year, his improvement is simply staggering. He is now an extremely proficient table tennis player, capable of playing in tournaments against experienced opposition.

This YouTube clip underlines the fact that anyone can make significant games with passion and commitment. However, it is also notable that the table tennis protagonist did not achieve his original aim of reaching a certain ranking in the UK. This succinctly illustrates the dichotomy between talent and practice. The latter will take you so far, but talent is a cherry on the cake which ultimately determines your potential.

Piotr Unierzyski's research suggests that the best tennis players possess natural genetic advantages. One is reminded of the prolific swimmer Michael Phelps, and the fact that his body produces less lactic acid than other people. His anatomy is literally built for swimming, and the top tennis players enjoy similar genetic advantages in their chosen profession.

Before any hand-eye coordination is taken into consideration, it should be noted that it is phenomenally difficult to get to the top in tennis if you are below a certain height. All of the top players in the men's game are over 6 foot tall. And many of the most successful female players are touching this figure as well. Unfortunately, if you are only 5' 8" in height, it will be difficult to be a professional tennis player. Not impossible, and you may have more fortune in the doubles sphere, but unfortunately if you are below average height that is an absolutely massive disadvantage.

Other genetic components also comprise your ultimate tennis potential, and unlike the author Matthew Syed - who suggest thats 10,000 hours of practice is the key to mastery in any field - I believe that you can only go so far without talent. Talent without perseverance is useless, perseverance alone will not get you to the very top. Sorry to be the bearer of bad news, but that's simply the reality of the situation.

However, I also believe that anyone can become a very proficient tennis player if they dedicate themselves to achieving this. The table tennis video certainly suggests that this is the case.

How Important is Practice?

You may have noticed by now that tennis is a game of repetition. Ultimately, entertaining though sport is to watch, most games are based on repetition. Achieving excellence is all about relentlessly training every aspect of your performance until it becomes second nature.

I would say that this is particularly true in a game such as tennis, in which, if all honesty, minimal strategy and tactics are involved. Much as though commentators like to talk tactics, and suggest that various players could try certain things on the match court, the reality is that almost all matches are decided by movement and the execution of strokes. Yes, there are certain things you can do on court to make your opponent uncomfortable, but there are no magic formulas available that will enable you to overcome hitting the ball badly.

This is why, in my opinion, tennis coaching is ultimately overrated. A tennis player must develop from their own experience. While this can be guided to a certain extent, there is no one out there that can teach you how to hit a tennis ball. No one taught Nadal his unique and devastating forehand; it simply developed from him hitting thousands and thousands of tennis balls. This applies to any stroke in the history of the game of tennis. You have to feel the ball onto the strings, and adjust your response to this feedback; much like driving a car.

I have a brief anecdote on this subject. A friend of mine is a chess grandmaster, and he sometimes coaches lesser players in an attempt to improve their level of play at the venerable board game. However, my friend firstly hates coaching, because he finds that lesser players often don't have the discipline or talent required to play at grandmaster level. And, secondly, he is actually unconvinced about the value of chess coaching whatsoever, as he points out that he himself received absolutely no coaching at all!

Unfortunately, there are no shortcuts in tennis either. Getting good at the game is all about drilling your shots day after day after day. At times it can get boring. That is something that you have to accept if you want to become a top class tennis player, and this is why I believe that love for the game is absolutely critical if you are to have any degree of success in reaching professional status. It is love for the sport that drags the likes of Federer, Nadal, Djokovic and Murray back to the practice court and gym time and time again, even after they have won so much and long since achieved financial independence.

Physical fitness is also tremendously important in the modern game of tennis, and it's hard to see how you can achieve this without massive commitment. You need to put in the hours in the gym, and you need to invest energy and commitment into the practice court. Taking on the tips and observations made in this blog will certainly make the process somewhat easier.

But ultimately your success and development as a tennis player is on you.

Talent Versus Application in the Professional Game

Another interesting question that is often asked is to what extent can application alone get you to a professional level in tennis. Can you become a world-class tennis player without any natural talent? And what exactly is natural talent anyway?

Natural talent can be something of a misleading concept. It seems somehow that a player with great elegance and spectacular shotmaking abilities, such as Roger Federer, must possess natural talent. But Federer himself will tell you that his particular skills have been honed in many thousands of hours spent on the practice courts. There are no shortcuts in the game of tennis, or in any professional sport, and in this sense all athletes are products of their environment.

However, it is difficult, if not completely stupid, to attribute the development of an athlete to environmental factors alone. There must be some intrinsic element to the performance of a player, something inside that separates the champion from the also-ran.

Yet Matthew Syed, in his book Bounce: The Myth of Talent and the Power of Practice, asserts that the main factor in the development of a professional proponent of any discipline is 10,000 hours of practice. Syed downplays the importance of genetic and inherited factors, citing several examples of professional players being agglomerated in favorable environments.

I certainly enjoyed Syed's book, yet I fundamentally disagree with him! However, where I would obviously agree with them is with regard to the importance of practice. This is clearly a critical aspect in any player's development, and I do believe that extraordinary things can be achieved with concerted training.

My personal definition of natural talent is that it represents the intrinsic potential that an individual possesses. This is incredibly hard to define, as many different factors can impact upon the performance of any sportsman or sportswoman. But it is obvious to me that different players have different degrees of potential, and what else can this be attributed to other than genetics, and ultimately natural talent?

My belief is that application without talent can absolutely get you to close to professional level. That's why I believe that following the tips in this book, and training with commitment, can help anyone, within reason, achieve a professional-standard of play. However, it is only sheer talent, intrinsic genetic potential, that will make you world-class. Those who do not possess this will plateau at a certain point, and never reach the heights of the ATP or WTA Tours.

This is profoundly illustrated by the careers of Roger Federer and David Ferrer. Everyone knows about Federer's staggering success, but David Ferrer has also been a particularly strong professional tennis player. The Spaniard has been ranked as high as three in the world, and has won millions of dollars of prize money, and several professional tournaments. He has undoubtedly been one of the best clay court players of his generation, and reached the French Open final back in 2013.

Yet Roger Federer has won 20 Grand Slam titles, and Ferrer has won zero. And the two players have met 17 times in the professional game, with Ferrer winning precisely zilch! Ferrer has had an absolutely outstanding career, by any reasonable standards, yet when measured against the very best, he quite clearly hasn't been quite good enough.

Considering that his work ethic is known to be absolutely outstanding, and, anyway, it is basically impossible to get to the top three in the world without a phenomenal level of practice and commitment, what else can this be attributed to other than pure natural talent? Federer is just intrinsically better than Ferrer. It's not about work ethic, it's not about practice, it's not about 10,000 hours of commitment. It's about talent.

You can manufacture a very decent and proficient tennis player, possibly even an ATP Tour professional, with hard work, practice, and dedication. But you can't make a champion. That just has to be inside you.

Chapter 8 - Mental Fitness, Physical Fitness and Advanced Drills

Before beginning this chapter, I should point out that I do not have any qualifications in sports psychology, nor do I have any experience in this field, aside from my own personal sporting attempts. However, I have studied psychology at university, and equally remain a keen student of how our psychological approach influences our view of the world, and at the way that we interact with it.

Equally, I'm not a personal trainer, but I feel the physical aspect of tennis is so important in the contemporary game that we must touch on it. This chapter will also look at some varied drills that you can engage in once you become an established and skilled proponent of the game of tennis.

It is certainly impossible to overlook the importance of psychology in tennis. If we take the two most successful male players of all time, Rafael Nadal and Roger Federer, it is clear that the latter suffered from psychological difficulties when meeting the former. Federer has even acknowledged this, stating that the number of defeats he suffered against Nadal on clay courts played a part in his overall losing record against the Spaniard. And, significantly, when Federer managed to break through this mental barrier recently, he was able to beat Nadal five times in a row for the first time in his career.

We all tend to judge the game of tennis in terms of forehands, backhands, winners and unforced errors. But there is plenty going on inside the mind and body of every tennis competitor during each match. There are very few games of tennis in which both competitors are in a position of psychological, mental and emotional equilibrium throughout the match, and also in which both players are free from any form of physical ailments.

Thus, those able to deal with the mental demands of tennis more readily and regularly will gain a massive advantage. This is obviously easier said than done, yet several techniques and observations have been established which make this process at least somewhat more achievable.

It's pretty much taken as a given that a positive mental attitude is essential in any sporting environment, or indeed to simply live up to one's potential in any field. But I think the other important aspect of tennis in a mental capacity is to focus on the process rather than the outcome. This is why I would place a particular emphasis on training and practice for younger players, as opposed to continual competition. Tournaments teach young players bad habits, whereas practice and training instil fundamentally good techniques.

The strong chess player and martial artist Joshua Waitzkin very much emphasizes this approach in his teaching. In both the push hands discipline at which he has become a world champion, and the game of chess in which he was also extraordinarily gifted, Waitzkin emphasizes a meticulous approach based around breaking down every single aspect of the sport, and studying them with great thoroughness.

I would not necessarily advocate this for young tennis players, as this can ultimately be draining and exhausting. But all great players have got good by endlessly working at the same strokes and drills, over and over again. Not by winning tournaments. Not by beating lesser players. Not by outhitting people with less power. Developing your game for the longer term should always be based on building your fundamentals, rather than racking up results. Once you have built these fundamentals, it is absolutely worthwhile to play more tournaments and try to obtain impressive results. Always begin with the basics.

I must say that when I played tennis competitively, I never utilized any form of mental approach. I just turned up and played. I considered myself to be mentally tough and to have good court craft (the latter, essentially an appreciation of what shots to play at what times, is notoriously difficult to teach). However, such techniques as visualization, relaxation and breathing techniques, and even meditation, are worth considering. The work of Dr. Steve Peters, in which he attempts to assist sports competitors with overcoming what he calls 'the chimp' is also worth looking at.

But, above all else, understand that everyone gets nervous, everyone gets tight, and everyone chokes. It doesn't matter who you are, how good you are, or how much you've won. Accept this, and if you fail mentally on one occasion then don't chastize yourself too much.

Developing Physically for Tennis

Muscular endurance is extremely important in tennis, and this is derived from an idealized combination of strength and endurance. When muscular endurance is developed, players gain the ability to perform repetitive actions over a longer period of time. We should have established by now that this is at the core of being a successful tennis player.

Tennis is an unusual sport in that it requires a combination of short-term and long-term endurance. Tennis matches can last for several hours, and are obviously split into a series of shorter and more explosive events. This means that your body needs the ability to cope with the several hours of play, but also with intense spurts of activity over a short period of time.

With this in mind, circuit training is ideal for tennis. This can include some intense activity, along with plenty of endurance work. Few professional tennis players lift a lot of heavy weights, but you can include some lifting in your routine, particularly as your body is developing. But being too top heavy is definitely not ideal for any tennis player, and can be seriously damaging to your body on hard courts in particular.

A foundational strength program can begin with exercises such as dumbbell squats, push ups, work on a stability ball, lunges, sit-ups, crunches with twists, dumbbell rows, shoulder presses, standing machine calf raises and barbell upright rows. These exercises work out your whole body, which is required in tennis. But you shouldn't be lifting massive weight for the weight-based exercises, rather you should be doing high numbers of reps with relatively liftable weights.

When building strength, you should look at doing barbell squats, lying leg presses, dumbbell bench presses, lat pull downs, dumbbell shoulder shrugs, bent over rows, and weighted crunches. These should be for a very small number of reps with heavier weights. You don't want to overdo the strength training as a tennis player, but undoubtedly some strength training is to be recommended.

Finally, the critical aspect of circuit training for a tennis player is endurance training. This should center around such exercises as squat jumps, side throws, hurdle jumps with sprint, over the back toss, box drill with rings, and slams. This can be done for high numbers of repetitions, and you should really push yourself to improve in this area. It is through doing these circuits that you build the capability to go from side to side, and then front and back, and then side to side some more, in long matches, for game after game after game. This will decide your fate as a tennis player just as much as your strokes.

Advanced Drills to Improve Your Tennis

I fundamentally believe that the basic drills discussed previously are the best way to develop your game. But as you become more technically proficient, you may begin to find these boring and uninspiring. So to mix things up for the proficient player, here is a list of various drills that you can carry out on a regular basis in order to become a better player.

Hitting Deep - a great place to begin with advanced drills is working on hitting with consistent depth. This is one of the critical aspects of playing tennis, particularly in the modern era in which virtually all play is from the baseline.

The aim of this particular drill is to land the ball between the service line and baseline on a regular basis. You can also choose to concentrate on the forehand or backhand, if you believe that one of these two groundstrokes needs particular work. But otherwise this is a straightforward drill, in which you hit dozens and dozens of balls, and score a point every time you hit the target area, losing a point when you hit the ball either long or short.

If you can score around 70 points from 100 balls then you're starting to become a strong player. This is another of those drills that requires patience, and hours of practice. But if you invest the time with hitting deep then you will develop a game ideally suited to long matches and tournaments.

Tramline Targets - to be honest with you, if you're out of form this game can be a little embarrassing! Even if you're a highly proficient player, hitting the tramline target can be extremely challenging. But it's also a great way to improve your accuracy, which is obviously of critical value in the game of tennis.

Tramline Targets involves simply playing within the tramlines of a tennis court. Aim every single shot that you hit within the tramlines, and use the same scoring system as for Hitting Deep. Again, if you feel that you particularly need to work on one of your groundstrokes then you can limit yourself to forehands or backends, but this drill is, quite honestly, tricky enough in itself. But that's no excuse for running around your backhand continually hitting forehands!

It could be argued that any positive score is a decent score, but strong players will aim to score around 40-50 from 100 balls. An easier version of this drill involves using just half the singles court, in which case a strong player would expect to score pretty much 100 out of 100.

Overhead Drill - the smash is probably the most spectacular stroke in tennis, but it is also one that is harder than it looks. Because it is a point finishing shot, there is often the feeling that it is necessary to hit overheads really hard, but this isn't actually the case. The smash can be a powerful and dramatic shot, but sometimes it is best to be a little conservative, and merely place it within the court.

Learning what type of overhead to use is best achieved by drilling it relentlessly. The overhead drill is witnessed in professional tennis all the time during the warmup, when the two players hit a series of smashes in order to practice the stroke. If you want to get really good at smashing then it is recommended to do hundreds and hundreds of repetitions in each overhead drill.

Possible variations with this drill include forcing yourself to take every ball out of the air without letting it bounce. But it is also worthwhile to learn from experience when it is better to let the ball bounce before attempting an overhead, so this can also form part of your practice routine. It is not a points-based drill; rather you should aim to hit every single overhead in the court and over the net. Harder than it sounds!

Return Drill - returning serve is another aspect of the game which causes problems at first. You simply have to train your eye to deal with the speed of the strong players' service motions. If you don't do this then you will never become a capable player. I recall the first time I faced an opponent with a really powerful serve, and it certainly takes some getting used to!

So the first way to work this particular drill is simply to stand behind the baseline in one corner of the court and receive dozens and dozens of serves from a strong opponent. There are also ball machines available which will mimic the service motion.

Alternate between training one particular return, and receiving serves within various parts of the service box. Train both your forehand and backhand, as the technique required to chip the ball back with a return is completely different to a driven groundstroke.

Some people have a natural acuity for this, but no matter how good you are initially at returning serve, the only way to reach professional standard is to practice and practice and then practice some more. Even if you have excellent reactions from another sport, you will be surprised to find that these aren't necessarily transferable into tennis.

Again, I would particularly recommend working on your backhand return, as powerful servers will snap your wrist back on the backhand side initially. You really need to train the wrist muscles as well as the stroke and motion itself.

Rapid Fire - this is one of the most fun drills that you can ever participate in on the tennis court, but it also trains your reactions and the proficiency of your groundstrokes and volleys. This is a drill that is ideally suited to a ball machine, but failing that a willing feeder and a bucket of balls can be equally effective.

The aim of this drill is to return as many balls back into court as possible in as short a time as conceivable! That's how it gets the name Rapid Fire! Set the ball machine on a rapid motion, or ask your playing partner to feed a large number of balls into the court in a short timeframe. And then simply return as many as you possibly can into the court.

It can be fun to keep a tally of your score here as well, but it is hard to say what represents a decent total. This really depends on the difficulty of the balls that you are fed. But not only is this a technical challenge, but it also gets the heart and blood pumping rapidly, so is really one of the most beneficial drills in the world of tennis.

Ball Drop - in a change of tack, this particular drill is intended to improve your footwork, and help you develop some of the skills that are vital in order to play tennis to a high standard. You can also make this drill more difficult by integrating exercises into the process as well.

Begin this drill crouched down at the side of the tennis court with five balls by your side. This drill involves four short shuttle runs. You have to place a ball on all four of the tramlines, as well as the centerline of the tennis court.

If you want to make it more difficult and particularly beneficial for yourself, then complete a circuit of exercises every time you return to collect a tennis ball. Squats, push-ups, star jumps, and burpees are all worthwhile exercises here.

Other ways of making it more difficult for yourself are by carrying weights inside your clothing during the process, and by also having to fetch the ball back to the side of the court at the end of the exercise. This is the most fun drill on the list, but it teaches you the sort of front and back motion that is so valuable in tennis, while also improving your fitness and footwork.

Half Court Match - this is a brilliant and simple way to improve your touch around the ntt, and was a particular favorite of mine when I played tennis competitively. I was always blessed with a decent touch with volleys, half volleys and drop shots, and I believe that this is partly because I participated in this drill as a young player.

The Half Court Match involves playing a standard tennis match within just the service box. As soon as you hit the ball beyond the service box, the point is over, as the service line represents the baseline in this form of the game. You can also only serve underarm.

There are no other rules in this form of tennis, apart from that it is played in exactly the same way as the standard version of the game. You can come to the net, or you can rely on groundstrokes. Either way, by playing this game on a regular basis you are really developing your touch, which can provide you with an extra string to your bow when you step on to the match court.

No Bounce Tennis - this is similar to Half Court Tennis, except that, as the name suggests, the ball is never permitted to bounce. You can really make your own rules regarding how this game works, but it is certainly advisable to play it in a shortened court, usually within the service box. The aim here is to improve your volleying, and it certainly has a beneficial effect on reaction time as well.

Rope Jumping - one of the best fitness exercises for tennis is skipping rope jumping. There are two obvious benefits to this. Firstly, it gets your heart going and is good for your aerobic fitness. And, secondly, it gets you on your toes, and improves the sort of movements that are typically utilized on the tennis court. If it's good enough for boxers, it's good enough for tennis players.

Split Step Practice - split steps are a critical tool in the tennis player's armory; you will notice that Roger Federer utilizes them with particular grace and elegance. This drill well help you develop your proficiency in split steps, and help you improve your movement on a tennis court.

Begin this drill at the back of the court behind the baseline, in the center of the court. Make the split step movement, and try to land slightly within the baseline.

Then run to the right hand side of the baseline, and repeat this motion. Then run back to the center of the court, and repeat it once more. Now run to the left-hand side of the court and repeat the motion on this side of the playing surface. Finally, return to the center of the court, and repeat the drill once again.

You should probably aim to do twenty repetitions of the drill just described in each session, although you can do more or less than this depending on your level of physical fitness.

Cones Drill - is another drill relating to movement, which will be extremely beneficial for your tennis development. Lay a series of cones around 8-feet apart in a W-shape on the court. The aim of this drill is to traverse through the cones as quickly as possible without stepping on them.

This one can be repeated around five times before taking a break, although if you're finding it too difficult then you should repeat the drill over and over again, having a break between each repetition. This then mirrors in the rhythms of tennis. But you should push yourself and get your heart rate going.

Dead Ball Drill - here is a classic drill that will turn you into the next Rafael Nadal if you get good at it!

For this drill, you either need an oscillating ball machine, or else a willing feeder. Begin in the center of the court, and have the ball fed to either your forehand or backhand to begin. The ball should be as close to the extremities of the singles court as possible. Run to the ball, return it with as much vigor as possible, and then return to the central position.

Then the feeder will hit the ball to the opposite corner of the court, and you then repeat the action from the first ball. You then repeat this motion over and over again; over a tennis training career this should be literally thousands of times.

The drill can be made more interesting by varying the corner to which balls are hits so that the player is unaware of which shot is coming next. Alternatively, the drill can literally done as forehand, backhand, forehand, backhand indefinitely, hammering home the relentless nature of high-quality baseline tennis.

Running Drive Drill - one of the critical aspects of tennis is the ability to hit the ball on the run. And this becomes more important as your game improves, and you begin to play again stronger players. You will notice that top class professional players are virtually as good as hitting the ball on the run, as they are at striking it from a stationary position. This is a key skill that you simply must muster in order to become a proficient competitor.

Equally, sometimes you are pushed so far out of the court that the only thing you can do is attempt to hit a winner. This can be achieved in one of two ways, either by powering the ball down the line, or by hitting an angled stroke across court. So the running drive drill tests both of these key aspects of a tennis player's armory.

The drill begins with a feeder taking up a position on the service line. The feeder will then send a ball into the forehand corner of the court, ensuring that it will be difficult to reach. For the purpose of this exercise, it isn't even really important for the ball to land legitimately in the court, what is vital is that the player participating in the drill is forced to run after it and ultimately hit a stroke while on the run.

Once reaching the ball, the player should either attempt to hit a powerful drive down the line, or a whipped topspin crosscourt winner. Once this has been attempted, the player will then return it to the center of the court. This drill then continues with the feeder putting the ball in both the forehand and backhand courts with roughly equal regularity. However, it is important that the player does not know which side that the ball will be fed, as the element of surprise is important in running it down and making the strike while on the run.

This drill can be repeated hundreds, and eventually thousands, of times, so that the player steadily improves this key aspect of the game.

Drop shot drill - Drop shots can be a key scoring stroke in the game of tennis, and therefore it is well worth practising them on a regular basis. Aside from anything else, drop shots often require the player to make an adjustment in grip, meaning that they can be a tricky part of the game.

This drop shot drill begins with players lining up across the service line, with the feeder positioned on the other side of the court. The ball will be fed into play, and the aim of the drill is to hit a drop shot that bounces three times before it reaches the service line. The ball should be fed to both forehand and backhand sides, so that the player can practice drop shots with both of their groundstrokes.

Combined with the drills that I've already mentioned in the book, these exercises will help develop all of the fundamental skills required to play tennis at a strong level. The only thing you need to do is commit yourself to them on a regular basis, and ensure that you always give 100% effort every time you step onto the practice court. With this attitude in place, your tennis is certain to progress sooner rather than later.

Chapter 9 – Examining the Success Stories

Ultimately, this book is intended to be a tool to assist any reader in getting the most out of their personal tennis talents. To some, this could even be reaching the very top of the game. So it would be foolish to end the text without examining some of the most notable success stories in the game of tennis. How did they develop, what did they do, what characterizes their rise to the top?

So this chapter will look at some of the most successful professional players, examining several with extremely diverse backgrounds and approaches to developing as juniors. It will discuss whether there is any wisdom in the approach of some of the most famous cases, and whether this can seriously be replicated.

The Model of the Williams Sisters

The story of Venus and Serena Williams is one of the best known in tennis, resulting in probably the greatest female tennis player in the history of the game. These two phenomenal athletes were born into relative poverty, and lived in the notorious Compton in Los Angeles, California. Yet while the upbringing of the sisters was not as underprivileged as has often been suggested, their tennis upbringing was rather unique.

Both of the Williams sisters were homeschooled from a young age, while their father was also strongly involved in their tennis coaching. Both of the Williams sisters attended the tennis academy of Rick Macci, but their father insisted on excluding them from national junior tennis tournaments as he wanted them to focus on their schoolwork. This really tallies with my belief that tournament play isn't remotely important when you're younger.

Venus and Serena were then pulled out of the Macci academy, and were then coached exclusively by their father until they entered the professional game. While tennis remained a big part of both of the sisters' lives, their development throughout adolescence took place outside of the mainstream system and USTA guidance. Support was always there, and the authorities absolutely understood just how good these two young players were. But the Williams sisters were raised differently to the norm.

Many credentialed observers asserted that this was completely misguided, and would lead to failure. 62 Grand Slam titles and 8 Olympic gold medals later, and I think we can safely say that the experts were wrong.

It is this operation outside of the mainstream system, and even competition, which makes the Williams sisters story so compelling. It should be said in mitigation that when you have two athletes of their caliber that it is an absolutely massive advantage. It would be rather stupid for anyone with two young girls to think that they could automatically coach them into the same level as the William sisters. This sort of story may never be repeated. Well, it probably won't be repeated!

But it does also illustrate that the conventional wisdom about bringing up a tennis player may be completely flawed. In fact, the way that Richard Williams chose to engage his daughters in tennis practice correlates quite strongly with my opinions. I believe that tournament play is pretty unimportant for young players, and that tennis should be a relatively small part of a young person's life, no matter how serious they may be about the game.

As stated in previous chapters, the story of the William sisters also demonstrates that tennis academies are by no means essential in the development of a player. Practice and enthusiasm for the game will ultimately be of far more value than some fancy and expensive institutions.

It should be said that Richard Williams pushed Venus and Serena far more than I believe to be ideal. This is by his own admission, incidentally. However, you could also argue that he has been entirely vindicated considering the level of tennis that they have produced, and is difficult to argue against this notion. Ultimately, I believe that the Williams sisters are the ideal illustration of how you can succeed in tennis with little money and minimal facilities; just like other sports that are generally considered to be more grassroots in nature.

How Nadal Became The Bull

Rafael Nadal was born in Manacor, Balearic Islands, Spain, and will forever be associated with the sun-soaked region. Nadal undoubtedly had an excellent grounding in professional sport, as his uncle, Miguel Ángel Nadal, played soccer for RCD Mallorca, FC Barcelona, and the Spanish national team. Indeed, many qualified observers believe that Rafa could have been a professional soccer player had he decided against pursuing tennis.

Nadal displayed talent in tennis from a young age, winning national titles by the age of eight. Yet it was around the age of 10 when the most interesting aspect of the young Nadal's development occurred. At this time, the Spaniard was coached exclusively by his uncle Toni, and his coach suggested that he radically change the way that he hit the tennis ball. Nadal had always used two hands on both groundstrokes, which is common for young players, yet Toni suggested using his left hand for the forehand instead.

This would hardly have been recommended by any professional coach whatsoever, as Nadal is right-handed. Yet by utilizing his left hand, Nadal developed one of the most feared forehands in the history of tennis. To say this would have gone against the coaching grain is a massive understatement, and it should also be emphasized that it would undoubtedly produce different results with another player. But this demonstrated that there is no right or wrong way of raising a young tennis player; every rule has an exception.

Nadal's career also underlines the fact that it is perfectly possible to achieve excellence outside of large academies. The Spanish Tennis Federation (La Real Federación Española de Tenis) requested for Nadal to leave Mallorca at the age of 14, and move to a big academy in Barcelona in order to continue tennis training. This would certainly have been the conventional route, but Nadal's family rejected this idea, instead placing an emphasis on education. Toni Nadal later commented that "I don't want to believe that you have to go to America, or other places to be a good athlete. You can do it from your home."

Just four years later, Nadal won the men's French Open singles title, so you'd have to say that this decision was vindicated!

Nadal certainly benefited from being brought up on clay, and it would be fascinating to know what sort of player he would have developed into with a different upbringing. But the key takeaway from his career is that, once again, it wasn't necessary to go the conventional route in order to become an outstanding player. Different strokes definitely work for different folks.

Other Notable Professional Upbringings

Two other absolutely world-class professional tennis players took a more conventional route to the top, but we can learn something from their experiences as well. Arguably the greatest of them all, Roger Federer, was inspired by watching Boris Becker win Wimbledon on television. Federer was eventually involved in some of Switzerland's top tennis academies, but it is his friendship with a contemporary that is perhaps most illuminating.

Federer met Marco Chiudinelli when he was just six years old, and the two have enjoyed an enduring friendship ever since. Both Federer and Chiudinelli were always ranked among the very top players in Switzerland from a young age, and competed in many representative squads together. Clearly the two youngsters went through extremely similar experiences, yet it was obvious from a young age that Federer simply had a special talent.

Adolf Kacovsky, a Czech tennis coach of Federer at The Old Boys Tennis Club in the Münchenstein principality of Switzerland, has been widely quoted as stating that Federer had immense natural talent. And while both Federer and Chiudinelli made it to the pros, the latter peaked just outside the top 50 in the world, never reaching the second week of a Grand Slam tournament, or reaching any singles final of note.

When Chiudinelli talks about his early experiences with Federer, it certainly sounds as if the two boys were soulmates. Yet one has become one of the world's greatest ever tennis players, while the other has enjoyed a decent, but ultimately moderate, professional career. Chiudinelli has nothing to be embarrassed about in terms of what he has achieved, and has reached much further than most people will ever achieve in the game. Surely the chasm between his career and that of Federer underlines the important aspect of a genetic component that simply cannot be taught with any amount of training.

Finally, to touch briefly on the ever controversial and notable career of Maria Sharapova, the Russian famously emigrated to the United States at a very young age. Her family made huge sacrifices in order to enrol her in the aforementioned IMG Academy of Nick Bollettieri, and despite massive language barriers, Sharapova ultimately flourished.

This does show that academies can work. And I suppose it also suggests that it is possible to craft a champion through sheer ambition. But it should be emphasized that the tale of Sharapova can be slightly misleading. A documentary of Sharapova, made for the television programme Trans World Sport, indicated that her father was hugely supportive or Maria, but, crucially never pushed her. Even from the age of eight or nine, much of the tennis ambition came from Sharapova herself, who was described by Bolletieri as an extremely precocious and confident person.

Rather than being molded into a champion, once again it seems that this quality was inherent in the young Sharapova. And when we examine the very top tennis players, time and time again we find that they had something inside them, something unique. Unfortunately, practice, hard work and sheer determination can take you so far, but I do believe that you need this elusive natural talent and drive if you want to become a true champion.

Conclusion

So what makes a good tennis player, what makes a great tennis player, what makes a champion tennis player, and how likely it is that you will achieve each of these levels with diligent effort and application?

In answering these questions, I'd like to begin this summary and conclusion of this book with two quotations from the most famous and garlanded tennis players in history. Roger Federer and Rafael Natal have been mentioned on several occasions in this book, because it is simply stupid and almost impossible to write a tennis book without discussing them. So let's mention them one last time!

I enjoyed the position I was in as a tennis player. I was to blame when I lost. I was to blame when I won. And I really like that, because I played soccer a lot too, and I couldn't stand it when I had to blame it on the goalkeeper. - Roger Federer

As a tennis player you can win and you can lose, and you have to be ready for both. - Rafael Nadal

These two quotes exemplify the biggest attraction of the game of tennis, and its greatest drawback. You alone are ultimately responsible for your performance on the court. There is no one else you can turn to, no other person to blame. It is perhaps why we often see professional players turning to their boxes with such regularity, as they are precisely seeking such an individual, when deep down they realize that there is no one to point the finger at for their performances other than themselves.

Equally, the pain of tennis is that you can invest a huge amount of effort, and lose horribly. Tennis is absolutely a zero sum game, there is always a winner and a loser. And every single tennis player that has ever played the game has always been a loser in the majority of tournaments that he or she has entered. You have to become accustomed to losing, and, as Kipling put it, treat the impostors of triumph and disaster just the same.

So your attitude towards the game of tennis will be central to fulfilling your potential. Someone once said to me that your ability to perform successfully in tennis tournaments is indicative of your level of independence and maturity. Considering that Nick Kyrgios is one of the world's best tennis players, I'm not sure that I would entirely endorse that statement! But I can certainly appreciate that opinion, and I think it is a view that has merit.

I'm not sure as an adolescent that I had the level of independence required to thrive as a tennis player. It was an awkward time in my life, as it is for many young people, and I didn't develop in the right way psychologically. There is no way I would have chosen to do what Andy Murray did; move away from home and live in Spain while still a teenager. From my perspective, it is only special, and essentially weird(!), people that will do this.

But what I am certain of is that to succeed in tennis, you have to be willing to take absolute responsibility for your own performance, and except that there will be many more troughs and disappointments than peaks. To return to the gentleman who played a part in the introduction of this book, Andrew Richardson won one only one professional tournament in his entire career. I'm sure he fondly remembers the Challenger in Urbana, United States, in which he beat Cecil Mamiit in the final. Even if no-one else but Mamiit does!

In short, in every single other week that Richardson participated in tennis during his professional career, he walked away a loser in some capacity. So accepting defeat is equally important in your development and quest to reach your potential. If you're going to excessively spit the dummy out every time you lose a tennis match, you're never going to enjoy the game, and I absolutely believe that enjoyment is allied to success.

Additionally, as I have mentioned previously, you have to to absolutely love playing tennis if you want to reach the upper echelons of the game. And I'm not even really talking about competing for Grand Slam titles, I really mean any sort of credible professional career whatsoever.

To give you an example, after the incredibly unlikely Wimbledon doubles victory of Jonathan Marray and Frederik Nielsen in 2012, the latter indicated that he would continue playing singles. This seems like a completely incomprehensible decision, as his earning potential as a doubles player after this wonderful and highly unexpected victory would have been far greater. But I absolutely understood the decision, as Nielsen realized that he is passionate about playing singles, and simply didn't want to give this up. No amount of tennis playing opportunities in doubles could compensate, and thus he was perfectly willing to give his doubles career away.

So I think fun should always be your priority at all times on the tennis court, at every level of the game. It can be difficult at times to enjoy tennis once you become competitive, and the game can certainly be hugely frustrating. But you should always try to remember why you began playing tennis in the first place, which should be because you enjoy hitting a tennis ball. If you cannot do this then your chances of sticking with the game for a prolonged period are extremely slim.

And this aspect of fun should always be allied to the principle of gradual and continual improvement. There will be many plateaus in your tennis playing career, and you have to be willing to push through these and make marginal gains. If you cannot do this then you will never have any chance of playing professional-standard tennis, as at a certain point, once you become a competent player, it will be difficult to significantly improve your strokes, certainly in a short period of time.

I strongly believe that there is a genetic component which ultimately decides the potential of every individual in every sport. And this cannot be overcome with any level of practice. However, if you wish to reach your ultimate potential then attitude will be far more important than any technical aspect. If you consistently demonstrate the right attitude to the game, and do the right things on court, rather than focusing on results, you may be surprised with how far your game develops.

Only by adopting this mindset can you ever hope to become tennis player 2.0.

You must also be realistic about what it is possible to achieve. However, I believe that it is possible for any player to produce professional-standard tennis. By this, I mean that anyone with a total dedication to the game, and applying anything remotely resembling a sensible approach to tennis, should be able to reach the top 1,000 players in the world.

This is based on my personal experience, and also the table tennis video that I mentioned earlier in the book. The level of improvement that the unskilled proponent of that video makes in one year, based on a persistent, and not excessive, program of practice suggests that massive improvements can be made over a longer period of time. I honestly believe that anyone starting young enough, with sufficient dedication, can play tennis at a very high level.

However, there is a world of difference between this and competing for ATP Tour titles. The only player which comes to mind who has managed to do this with moderate natural talent is the British female Jo Konta. This is massive credit to her determination and sheer love of the game, but most people who pick up a tennis racket and discover that they have mediocre talent should not expect to reach this standard.

So let me finish this book by telling you my story. I quit playing tennis seriously as a teenager, and didn't pick up a racquet again for 20 years, although I watched tennis extensively, and remained a fan of the sport. When I quit playing, I was ranked in the top 20 players in my age group in Britain, I'd played in the National Finals of short tennis, clay court tennis, hard court tennis and grass court tennis, and also in the British Schools finals. When I gave up the game, all of the coaches I'd worked with at the LTA were really disappointed, believing it to be a waste of talent. So why did I do it?

Two reasons. Firstly, I didn't believe for one second that I could become as good as the star of the introduction to this book! Andrew Richardson was a phenomenal tennis player, I played with him every week and observed this, and I don't think I could ever have reached his level. I think my genetic peak was somewhere below this.

I was quite a smart teenager, and already I could see my future trekking around the Challenger tournaments of Tashkent and Astana, trying to make enough money to be able to afford a hotel room, before losing in the second round to the world number 347. I figured that I should probably look for a career in which I would actually make money instead, much though it's a nice dream to think that you'll end up on the Wimbledon honours board.

And, more importantly, I was bored of playing tennis by this age. I didn't hate it, but I didn't love it enough to even begin to want to trek around Kazakhstan and Uzbekistan. It was a nice novelty to be really good at something when I was younger, but the novelty had worn off. I had proved I could play tennis, and I didn't want to put in another 5,000 hours practice, in the vain hope of improving my play by mere fractions.

I didn't love tennis like Andy Murray does. I didn't enjoy competing like Lleyton Hewitt did. And you need that love of the game to fulfil your potential, not that I believe my genetic potential was good enough to be a notable player. I might have scraped into the top 200 with an unbelievable amount of effort, but I was never going to be a superstar. At my peak, I could beat 99% of players of my age without difficulty. But this isn't necessarily good enough.

Finally, I would also like to mention to all parents reading this book that my parents were extremely understanding when I made the decision to quit. This is despite the fact that my father had invested a vast amount of time in driving me all over the country, and a significant amount of money had also been spent on my tennis career. We were not exactly impoverished, but we were also not a wealthy family, so I now appreciate the sacrifices that my parents made in order for me to be able to play tennis at the high-level.

Yet not only was I never pushed, as was mentioned earlier in the book, but when I decided to quit, there was absolutely no resistance to this whatsoever. My mother and father absolutely accepted my decision, simply taking a little time to talk it over with me, and ensure that I was happy with this decision.

It is certainly not a decision that I regret or have regretted, as I learnt enough during my years in the game to appreciate that not many young players make it, despite the often massive investment of energy, money and time that both they and their parents make. And many young players ultimately end up feeling resentful towards the game of tennis, and even hating it, precisely because they are pushed, or even coerced, into participating in the sport.

And I really want to warn parents who are reading this text to understand that this sort of conduct never ends well. You will not create a champion, nor a well-adjusted human being, just because you want your children to be successful. Do not push them into playing tennis. The decision to play has to emanate from them, all you can do is support them. And if they have talent but choose to walk away, I hope you can accept this with the responsibility and maturity that my parents showed.

Ultimately, I hope this book is a guide to being the best tennis player or parent that you can be, and that it also helps you understand and remember something the next time that you see Federer routinely pasting the world number 37 at Wimbledon.

The world number 37 is an extremely special person just to be there in the first place.

About the Expert

Christopher Morris was ranked in the top 20 juniors in Britain in both short tennis and lawn tennis as a teenager. He was also part of the first state school team to reach the British schools finals. An insider in the British LTA scheme, Morris was part of several of the top junior development squads, where he regularly played against several players, both male and female, who went on to play professional tennis. He also worked with the highest rated LTA coaches of the time.

Morris has since become a successful freelancer writer, with his work featuring in Newsweek, Yahoo and Seeking Alpha, amongst many other publications. His personal website is christopherpaulmorris.com

HowExpert publishes quick 'how to' guides on all topics from A to Z by everyday experts. Visit HowExpert.com to learn more.

Recommended Resources

- <u>HowExpert.com</u> – Quick 'How To' Guides on All Topics by Everyday Experts.
- <u>HowExpert.com/books</u> – HowExpert Books
- <u>HowExpert.com/products</u> – HowExpert Products
- <u>HowExpert.com/courses</u> – HowExpert Courses
- <u>HowExpert.com/clothing</u> – HowExpert Clothing
- <u>HowExpert.com/membership</u> – Learn All Topics from A to Z by Real Experts.
- <u>HowExpert.com/affiliates</u> – HowExpert Affiliate Program
- <u>HowExpert.com/jobs</u> – HowExpert Jobs
- <u>HowExpert.com/writers</u> – Write About Your #1 Passion/Knowledge/Expertise.
- <u>YouTube.com/HowExpert</u> – Subscribe to HowExpert YouTube.
- <u>Instagram.com/HowExpert</u> – Follow HowExpert on Instagram.
- <u>Facebook.com/HowExpert</u> – Follow HowExpert on Facebook.

CPSIA information can be obtained
at www.ICGtesting.com
Printed in the USA
LVHW081207171219
640783LV00010B/60/P